From Imperialism
to Isolationism

1898–1919

NEW PERSPECTIVES
IN AMERICAN HISTORY

Donald B. Cole, *editor*
The Phillips Exeter Academy

Henry W. Bragdon
Samuel P. McCutchen
co-editors

From Imperialism to Isolationism

1898–1919

ERNEST R. MAY

Harvard University

The Macmillan Company, New York
Collier-Macmillan Limited, London

ACKNOWLEDGMENTS

For permission to quote copyright material, the author is grateful to the following:

Abelard-Schuman, Ltd.: For an excerpt from *The Isolationist Impulse* by Selig Adler. Reprinted by permission of Abelard-Schuman, Ltd., New York, London, Toronto.

Samuel F. Bemis: For an excerpt from *Diplomatic History of the United States* by Samuel F. Bemis. Published by Holt, Rinehart & Winston, Inc.

Charles Lauriat: For excerpts from *The Lusitania's Last Voyage* by Charles Lauriat; poem by William L. Garrison in *The Lusitania's Last Voyage* by Charles Lauriat. Published by Houghton Mifflin Company.

Arthur Link: For an excerpt from *Wilson, The Diplomatist* by Arthur Link. Published by The Johns Hopkins Press.

Alfred A. Knopf, Inc.: For an excerpt from *The Growth of American Foreign Policy* by Richard Leopold. Published by Alfred A. Knopf, Inc.

The Macmillan Company: For excerpts from *The Idea of National Interest* by Charles Beard; *Woodrow Wilson and the Great Betrayal* by Thomas Bailey. Reprinted by permission of The Macmillan Company.

✓ ✓ ✓

FOR MAMA DONNA

✓ ✓ ✓

Contents

Intervention in Cuba: 1898

On the evening of February 15, 1898, the United States battleship *Maine* was riding quietly at anchor in Havana harbor. Taps had sounded. No one was on deck except the evening watch and a few officers sitting aft smoking. Captain Charles Sigsbee, in his cabin, was reading the letter he had just written his wife. Suddenly from the port side came a terrific roar. Watchers on the shore saw a column of fire rise into the sky. All at once the forward part of the ship was an inferno, with burning fragments raining down, cartridges in the ammunition lockers exploding and whizzing about, and men running frantically, screaming with pain. Rushing topside, Sigsbee saw the bow already beginning to settle. He ordered "Abandon ship." Ninety-eight men went over the side, Sigsbee last of all. In the burning wreckage remained 252 dead.

In other circumstances the destruction of the *Maine* might have been, like the later sinking of the *Titanic*, a sea

1

disaster to be remembered solely because of the hideous loss of life. But the circumstances were not normal. Cuba was a Spanish colony. Relations between the United States and Spain had been troubled for nearly three years, and in both countries there were already people calling for war. The explosion of the *Maine* seemed an incident that might touch off such a war.

In Cuba a revolution for independence was raging. From its beginning in 1895, it had had support from sympathizers in the United States. The shipping of arms and the recruiting of volunteers were forbidden by international law, and the American government tried to stop such overt aid. But its efforts were unsuccessful. The Atlantic coast had too many bays and inlets from which ships could slip out in the night. More important, public sentiment was with the lawbreakers rather than with the government. No one would inform on contraband runners. Even when they were caught red-handed, juries would sometimes acquit them with congratulations. From the Spanish standpoint it seemed as if all Americans were allies of the Cuban rebels. Suspecting that the United States wanted Cuba for itself, many Spaniards regarded Americans as their real enemies. Some thought it would be better if war were openly declared.

Regarding the United States government, these Spaniards were wrong. Grover Cleveland, who was President until 1897, said firmly and repeatedly that he did not think Cuba could or should be incorporated into the union. William McKinley, who succeeded him, considered financiers and industrialists the best judges of what was good for the country. Knowing that most such men opposed war with Spain, largely on the ground that it would interrupt recovery from the existing economic depression, McKinley was intent on keeping the peace.

But the government was one thing and the public was another. From almost the first day of the Cuban revolution, people throughout the United States followed it with intense interest. Cuban agents waged a propaganda campaign, and

863,956
WORLDS CIRCULATED YESTERDAY
" Circulation Books Open to All."

The World.

" Circulation Books Open to All."

863,956
WORLDS CIRCULATED YESTERDAY

VOL. XXXVIII. NO. 13,339.   NEW YORK, THURSDAY, FEBRUARY 17, 1898.   PRICE

MAINE EXPLOSION CAUSED BY BOMB OR TORPEDO?

Capt. Sigsbee and Consul-General Lee Are in Doubt---The World Has Sent a Special Tug, With Submarine Divers, to Havana to Find Out---Lee Asks for an Immediate Court of Inquiry---260 Men Dead.

IN A SUPPRESSED DESPATCH TO THE STATE DEPARTMENT, THE CAPTAIN SAYS THE ACCIDENT WAS MADE POSSIBLE BY AN ENEMY.

Dr. E. C. Pendleton, Just Arrived from Havana, Says He Overheard Talk There of a Plot to Blow Up the Ship---Capt. Zalinski, the Dynamite Expert, and Other Experts Report to The World that the Wreck Was Not Accidental---Washington Officials Ready for Vigorous Action if Spanish Responsibility Can Be Shown---Divers to Be Sent Down to Make Careful Examinations.

DRAWN FROM A DESCRIPTION BY EYE-WITNESSES ON THE STEAMSHIP CITY OF WASHINGTON WHO SAW THE EXPLOSION, FOLLOWED BY "A VOLCANO OF FIRE AND SHOWERS OF BOATS, BODIES, IRON AND GUNS," CABLED TO THE WORLD BY ITS OWN CORRESPONDENT IN HAVANA. SYLVESTER SCOVEL.

THE WHOLE STORY OF THE DISASTER TOLD IN A FEW WORDS.

some newspaper publishers helped them. In New York Joseph Pulitzer's *World* and William Randolph Hearst's *Journal* were engaged in a circulation war. Finding that lurid writing about the Cuban civil war helped to sell newspapers, Pulitzer and Hearst not only made the most of what came to hand but sometimes created stories of their own. Hearst, for example, publicized the plight of Evangelina Cisneros, an eighteen-year-old Cuban girl imprisoned in Havana. Then, through one of his correspondents, he engineered her escape to the United States and a triumphal reception for her in New York.

But rebel propagandists and such journalists as Hearst and Pulitzer merely took advantage of the public's interest; they did not create it. Even if reported accurately, conditions in Cuba would still have awakened passionate concern among Americans. The long-continued fighting ravaged the sugar plantations that were the backbone of the island's economy, driving tens of thousands from their homes and farms and reducing the whole population to misery. Trying desperately to combat the rebels, the Spaniards made conditions worse. General Valeriano Weyler, whose nickname in the Spanish army was "Butcher," resorted to *reconcentración*—removing all the people from rural districts, reconcentrating them behind the Spanish lines, and then, in hope of starving the rebels out, destroying all fields and farms. Little or nothing was left for the poor *reconcentrados* to eat. Accounts of their plight were heart-rending, and, reading them, many Americans felt that their government ought to do something to stop the suffering.

Most thought that the government should aid the rebels. The conflict in Cuba was between a European monarchy and colonists seeking to establish an independent republic. Given their own history, Americans naturally took the side of the colonists. Because the monarchy in question was Spain, their sympathies were all the stronger. Spain was still thought of by most Americans as a medieval land where the Inquisition tortured heretics and burned non-Catholics at the stake. America was then pronouncedly Protestant; anti-Catholicism was strong; and many American Protestants were willing, indeed eager, to believe the worst of all Spaniards.

As early as the winter of 1895 there had been large public demonstrations in favor of intervention in Cuba. In 1896 came still larger ones. Responding to public pressure, Congress voted a resolution urging the executive branch to take action. When Cleveland failed to do anything, Senators and Representatives threatened to pass another, stronger resolution, one that would have the force of law and would compel the executive to act.

When McKinley succeeded Cleveland, public feeling quieted for a time. McKinley pressed the Spanish government to grant Cuba dominion status, such as Canada enjoyed in the British Empire. Having already decided to try such a scheme, Spanish officials agreed and started proceedings to establish some degree of home rule. Although the rebels refused to compromise and nearly all observers predicted that home rule would not succeed, many Americans seemed willing to wait and see what happened.

Then, however, came 1898. January saw anti-American riots in Havana. In early February, a private letter written by the Spanish minister to the United States, Enrique Dupuy de Lôme, was stolen from the mails and published. Not only did it speak of McKinley in uncomplimentary terms, but it suggested that the Spanish government had not been negotiating in good faith. Then, only a few days later, the *Maine* blew up. Little wonder that people on both sides began to ask, "Was she deliberately blown up? Is this the beginning of war?"

To reporters and Congressmen who clamored for a statement, McKinley answered soothingly that a full investigation would be made and that afterward the government would take whatever steps seemed necessary. Supporting him, bankers and lawyers, many ministers, and a large number of newspaper editors called for calm and forbearance.

But within two weeks a kind of hysteria began to sweep the land. No one knew what had caused the *Maine* explosion. Indeed, no one knows to this day. Conceivably, reckless Spanish fanatics were to blame. More probably, a harbor mine accidentally came unanchored and drifted into contact with the hull, or a spark aboard ship touched off the powder magazine. In any case, there can be no doubt whatever that the Spanish government did not deliberately order its destruction. Every responsible person in Madrid knew that war with the United States would end disastrously for Spain. Many people in the United States were nevertheless prepared to believe the Spanish government at fault, and there was loud clamor for revenge.

New mass demonstrations broke out in many cities. In country towns it was the same. One observer reported ruefully, "Everything is war talk . . . , and patriotism is oozing out of every boy who is old enough to pack feed to the pigs." People began to condemn McKinley for doing nothing. Before long, his picture was being hissed in theaters, and effigies of him were burned during war rallies.

Neither he nor those around him could long hold out against such fervor. In Congress on March 17 Senator Redfield Proctor of Vermont, an erstwhile opponent of intervention, reported on a recent trip to Cuba. The *reconcentrados*, he said, lived in

> huts . . . about 10 by 15 feet in size, and for want of space are usually crowded together very closely. They have no floor but the ground, no furniture, and, after a year's wear, but little clothing except such stray substitutes as they can extemporize; and with large families, or more than one, in this little space, the commonest sanitary provisions are impossible. Conditions are unmentionable in this respect. Torn from their homes, with foul earth, foul air, foul water, and foul food or none, what wonder that one-half have died and that one-quarter of the living are so diseased that they cannot be saved?

Proctor said that he had gone to Cuba "with a strong conviction that the picture had been overdrawn; that a few cases of starvation and suffering had inspired and stimulated the press correspondents, and that they had given free play to a strong, natural, and highly cultivated imagination." But what he had seen with his own eyes convinced him that this was not the case. "To me," he concluded, "the strongest appeal is not . . . the loss of the *Maine*, if our worst fears should prove true, . . . but the spectacle of a million and half of people, suffering from the worst misgovernment of which I ever had knowledge. . . ." He indicated that he would now vote in favor of intervention.

Many other erstwhile administration supporters followed Proctor's lead. Soon it was apparent that if McKinley did not act, Congress might, on its own initiative, declare war.

In near desperation, McKinley appealed to the Queen Regent of Spain. Warning that Congress was almost out of hand, he asked her to order an end to reconcentration, to proclaim an armistice in Cuba, and to give him a guarantee that fighting would not be resumed—even if Spain had to grant the island independence.

After long, tortured debate within the cabinet, the Spanish government agreed to all but one of these conditions. The Queen ended reconcentration and directed Spanish forces to cease fire. She would not, however, guarantee the permanence of the peace. Concerned above all with preventing a republican revolution in Spain, she felt that the monarchy could more easily survive an unsuccessful war with the United States than it could a charge that it had given up Cuba on account of cowardice.

From McKinley's standpoint, the Spanish concessions were not enough. He, too, was afraid of revolution. In 1896, he had narrowly defeated William Jennings Bryan, the champion of free coinage of silver. To him and most Republicans, Bryan and his platform had seemed wildly radical. Now the Cuban issue united many of Bryan's followers with others who had not been captivated by free silver. The Chicago *Times-Herald*, a leading Republican organ in the Midwest, declared,

"Intervention in Cuba . . . is immediately inevitable. Our own internal political conditions will not permit its postponement. Who that has marked the signs of the times does not see that 'war for Cuban liberty' looms before us as the only rallying standard of the legions of our national discontent."

Had McKinley been able to promise that warfare would not resume in Cuba, he might have felt that he could ask Congress and the public to be patient. Had he been a braver man, he might have tested whether or not Congress would wait to see what came of the concessions Spain had made. As it was, he decided to yield to the public demand for war.

On April 11 he went before Congress. Although saying that responsibility for the *Maine* disaster was still not fixed, he continued:

> In any event the destruction of the *Maine*, by whatever exterior cause, is a patent and impressive proof of a state of things in Cuba that is intolerable. That condition is thus shown to be such that the Spanish Government can not assure safety and security to a vessel of the American Navy in the harbor of Havana on a mission of peace, and rightfully there. . . .
>
> The long trial has proved that the object for which Spain has waged the war can not be attained. The fire of insurrection may flame or may smolder with varying seasons, but it has not been, and it is plain that it can not be extinguished by present methods. The only hope of relief and repose from a condition which can no longer be endured is the enforced pacification of Cuba. In the name of humanity, in the name of civilization, in behalf of endangered American interests which give us the right and the duty to speak and to act, the war in Cuba must stop.
>
> In view of these facts and of these considerations, I ask the Congress to authorize and empower the President to take measures to secure a full and final termination of hostilities between the Government of Spain and the people of Cuba, and to secure in the island the establishment of a stable government, capable of maintaining order and observing its international obligations, insuring peace and

tranquility and the security of its citizens as well as our own, and to use the military and naval forces of the United States as may be necessary for these purposes. . . .

On April 19 Congress voted the authority McKinley had asked, demanding in addition that Spain relinquish sovereignty over Cuba. McKinley put this demand before Spain in a formal ultimatum. When the Spaniards rejected it, the United States and Spain were at war.

Historians have disagreed about the reasons for this war. Some who wrote soon after the event were convinced that sinister economic interests had been responsible. It was the heyday of the trust; the McKinley administration was very much pro-business; the war made money for the steel trust, the oil trust, the meatpacking trust, and the sugar trust; and these historians surmised that big business must have planned it so. Not until 1936, when Julius W. Pratt published *Expansionists of 1898*, was it proved beyond dispute that businessmen, big and little, had foreseen nothing but evil and had opposed war almost to the end.

Meanwhile, other historians had come up with other villains. Public opinion had forced the government's hand, they said, but public opinion had been whipped up by Hearst, Pulitzer, and other publishers of inflammatory "yellow journals." Although this verdict has not been overturned so decisively, it, too, has failed to stand the test of time. More recent scholarship has found that the war fervor extended far beyond the subscription areas of these newspapers; it arose at a time when people's minds were already unsettled by the changeover from a farming to an industrial society. At the same time, however, it was a good deal more rational than earlier students had conceded: hundreds of thousands were dying in Cuba in a war that neither side appeared likely to win and that only the United States could end, and Americans felt that intervention was a moral duty. Today the causes of the war seem much more complex than they once did; and future scholars may find that the complexities are even greater than we now imagine.

One thing that seems clear is that the war did not come because Americans wanted new territory. The war of 1812 had been affected, if not caused, by the desire of some to conquer Canada and Florida. The conflict with Mexico in the 1840's had had behind it a hunger for western land and ports on the Pacific. But in 1898 almost no champion of intervention advocated taking or keeping any part of the Spanish empire. When voting for intervention in Cuba, Congress accepted the Teller Amendment, which declared explicitly: "The United States hereby disclaims any disposition or intention to exercise sovereignty, jurisdiction, or control over said island, except for the pacification thereof, and asserts its determination, when that is accomplished, to leave the government and control of the island to its people."

Yet, paradoxically, the war that began in such a spirit ended in a matter of months with the United States taking from Spain the largest part of her empire. Having been for a hundred and twenty-two years the world's leading champion of independence for colonial people, the nation suddenly became itself a colonial power. How did this happen?

Imperialism

The turning point came less than three months after the *Maine's* mishap, when another American warship, the *Olympia*, put into a harbor over 7,000 miles away. The war was now on. The *Olympia*, with Commodore George Dewey aboard, was flagship for the six-vessel American Asiatic Squadron. It was sailing under orders to find Spain's Pacific fleet and, if possible, to destroy it.

When drawn up in Washington, these orders had seemed more or less routine. Later the story was to be told that Secretary of the Navy John D. Long took a holiday, leaving in charge his ebullient Assistant Secretary, Theodore Roosevelt. An advocate of national expansion, Roosevelt saw a chance to stage-manage a clash with Spain in the Pacific, the result of which might be that the United States would take over Spain's Pacific empire. To this end he sent off the orders to Dewey.

What actually happened was that Roosevelt, more eager for war than was his chief, sent out a number of dispatches that were not supposed to go out until war was nearer at hand. The one to Dewey happened to be among these. Although most of the Spanish navy was in the Atlantic and the really important naval battles were expected there, nine ships were known to be stationed at Spain's Philippine colony. If left alone, they might attack American shipping in the Pacific or even raid the United States west coast. It was only logical that, when war began, the American Asiatic Squadron should

11

sail as fast as possible for Manila in hope of catching some or all of them before they took to the high seas.

A no-nonsense sailor whose vessels were already in fighting trim, Dewey made for the port at top speed. In the early hours of May 1, when he passed through the narrows into Manila Bay, with Corregidor Island to port, all nine of the Spanish ships were still there. Engaging them at daybreak and fighting on until past noon, he sank or put out of action every one—with not a single American killed! What might have been a minor action thus turned out to be a spectacular triumph. The news caused Americans to swell with pride. It also made many feel that a sign had come from Providence.

Up to that time America had had relatively few imperialists. England had many. So did France, Germany, and Russia. In each of those countries prominent political leaders advocated building colonial empires. Some took the ground that colonies were needed to provide raw materials for factories and markets for the factories' fast-growing output. Others used military and naval arguments, saying that colonies would supply manpower for armies or serve as bases from which warships could cut an enemy's supply lines. Still others contended simply that colonies were emblems of national status and that to have them was to have one's "place in the sun." Between the 1870's and the 1890's European governments carved up Africa and established spheres of influence in the Middle East and Asia, but the United States did not take part nor even pay much attention to what they were doing.

In the late 1880's and early 1890's a few imperialist voices had risen in America. John Fiske, a popularizer of Darwinism, gave public lectures arguing that now the "manifest destiny" of America was to spread to other parts of the globe. The Reverend Josiah Strong, a leader in the Congregational Church, presented the same case more passionately in sermons, articles, and books. Alfred Thayer Mahan, a captain in the navy, reached a wide audience with his thesis that America would fall behind other nations unless it looked to its sea power, and he claimed that sea power entailed overseas colonies. But even Mahan was better received abroad than at home. It was in England and Germany rather than the United States that he was most acclaimed and that his books enjoyed their liveliest sale. Before 1898 there was little indication that arguments such as Fiske's, Strong's, and Mahan's had had much impact on the American public.

There was, it is true, a movement for annexing the Hawaiian islands. A number of Americans had settled there, and in 1893 they staged a successful revolution against the native government and appealed to the United States to take the islands as a territory. At first the public seemed to approve, but when President Cleveland rejected annexation, there was little popular outcry. Some Republicans attacked the decision, a few in terms suggesting that they favored a general policy of acquiring colonies. Until 1898, however, they were very few. The only two with national reputations were Theodore Roosevelt and Massachusetts Senator Henry Cabot Lodge.

Dewey's triumph at Manila Bay changed all this. Suddenly politicians, newspaper editors, businessmen, clergymen— leaders of opinion in every walk of life—discovered that the nation had an imperial destiny. Not realizing that the Spaniards had an army as well as a fleet in the Philippines, most people assumed that Dewey's victory put the islands in American hands. Believing that Spanish administration had been as bad there as in Cuba, they felt almost unanimously that sovereignty should not be returned to Spain. The alternatives seemed to be to turn the islands over to another European power, to set up an independent native government, or to annex the Philippines as a colony. A large number concluded not only that annexation was the right choice but that, in general, the nation ought to change its policy and become a colonial power. An imperialist movement suddenly flowered.

Within weeks after Dewey's victory, Congress voted to annex Hawaii. When military operations in the Caribbean extended to Puerto Rico, Spain's one other possession in the

Western Hemisphere, voices arose saying that, while the United States had promised to give up Cuba, it ought to keep the smaller island. And speeches and editorials by the hundreds urged McKinley, in regard to the Philippines, to consider no alternative to annexation.

With the congressional election campaign under way, the pros and cons of Philippine annexation were debated in forums all over the country. By and large, the younger men in the Republican party were the most ardent champions of an imperial policy. None was more so than thirty-five-year-old Albert J. Beveridge, an Indiana lawyer who aspired to a seat in the United States Senate (and was to win it). In a speech at Indianapolis in September, 1898, he put the case for imperialism in passionate rhetoric. Under the title "The March of the Flag," this speech was reprinted and used throughout the nation as a campaign document. It remains the arch-typical statement of the imperialist creed.

Beveridge started from three assumptions then common. The first was that there were distinctive races such as Anglo-Saxon, Teutonic, Latin, and Slavic and that there were differences in quality among them. The second was that, of these, the Anglo-Saxon race was the best (the proof being England's industrial and financial might, the extent of her empire, and the success of her colonists as compared with others). The third was that, in spite of the influx of immigrants from other lands, the United States remained predominantly Anglo-Saxon in race and institutions. Said Beveridge:

> It is a noble land that God has given us . . . , a greater England with a nobler destiny.
> It is a mighty people that He has planted on this soil; a people sprung from the most masterful blood of history; a people perpetually revitalized by the virile, man-producing working-folk of all the earth; a people imperial by virtue of their power, by right of their institutions, by authority of their Heaven-directed purposes—the propagandists and not the misers of liberty.

Those who opposed an imperial policy argued that the tradition of the United States was isolationist. Washington in his Farewell Address had counseled "as little *political* connection as possible" with other nations. The Monroe Doctrine had proclaimed the interests of the United States confined to the Western Hemisphere. Anti-imperialists appealed to these hallowed documents. But Beveridge disputed their claim to the sanction of history. He asserted that the actual tradition of the nation was expansionist, that ". . . we do but what our fathers did—we but pitch the tents of liberty farther westward, farther southward—we only continue the march of the flag." Reminding his hearers of the Louisiana Purchase, the acquisition of Florida, the annexation of Texas, and the Mexican War, Beveridge declaimed:

The march of the flag! In 1789 the flag of the Republic waved over 4,000,000 souls in thirteen states, and their savage territory which stretched to the Mississippi, to Canada, to the Floridas. The timid minds of that day said that no new territory was needed. . . . But Jefferson, through whose intellect the centuries marched; . . . Jefferson, the first Imperialist of the Republic—Jefferson acquired that imperial territory which swept from the Mississippi to the mountains, from Texas to the British possessions, and the march of the flag began! . . .

A screen of land from New Orleans to Florida shut us from the Gulf, and over this and the Everglade Peninsula waved the saffron flag of Spain; Andrew Jackson seized both, the American people stood at his back, and, under Monroe, the Floridas came under the dominion of the Republic, and the march of the flag went on! The Cassandras prophesied every prophecy of despair we hear, to-day, but the march of the flag went on!

Then Texas responded to the bugle calls of liberty, and the march of the flag went on! And, at last, we waged war with Mexico, and the flag swept over the southwest, over peerless California, past the Gate of Gold to Oregon on the north, and from ocean to ocean its folds of glory blazed.

And, now, obeying the same voice that Jefferson heard and obeyed, that Jackson heard and obeyed, that Monroe

heard and obeyed, . . . our President to-day plants the flag
over the islands of the seas, outposts of commerce, citadels
of national security, and the march of the flag goes on!

Beveridge did not appeal only to history and to the
mystique of race. In the United States as in western Europe
industrial production had rapidly expanded. Manufacturers,
financiers, and other businessmen had begun to worry that production would outstrip consumption; the day might come when
factories would continue to turn out goods but there would be
no one to buy them; the whole system might collapse. Territorial expansion, Beveridge contended, could lay this dread
to rest:

> We did not need the western Mississippi Valley when
> we acquired it, nor Florida, nor Texas, nor California,
> nor the royal provinces of the far northwest. We had no
> emigrants to people this imperial wilderness, no money
> to develop it, even no highways to cover it. No trade
> awaited us in its savage fastnesses. Our productions were
> not greater than our trade. There was not one reason for
> the land-lust of our statesmen from Jefferson to Grant,
> other than the prophet and the Saxon within them. But,
> to-day, we are raising more than we can consume, making
> more than we can use. Therefore we must find new markets
> for our produce.
> And so, while we did not need the territory taken
> during the past century at the time it was acquired, we do
> need what we have taken in 1898, and we need it now.
> The resources and the commerce of these immensely rich
> dominions will be increased as much as American energy
> is greater than Spanish sloth. . . .
> The riches of the Philippines have hardly been touched
> by the finger-tips of modern methods. And they produce
> what we consume, and consume what we produce. . . .
> They sell hemp, sugar, cocoanuts, fruits of the tropics,
> timber of price like mahogany; they buy flour, clothing,
> tools, implements, machinery and all that we can raise and
> make. Their trade will be ours in time.

And profit and glory, Beveridge said, would go hand in
hand. European imperialists used the phrase "place in the sun."

From " The Rocky Mountain News," Denver, 1900.

Uncle Sam: "By gum, I rather like your looks."

Beveridge went beyond them. If America followed an imperial-ist policy, he declared, it could aspire to dominance:

> The commercial supremacy of the Republic means that this Nation is to be the sovereign factor in the peace of the world. For the conflicts of the future are to be con-flicts of trade—struggles for markets—commercial wars for existence. And the golden rule of peace is impregnability of position and invincibility of preparedness. So, we see Eng-land, the greatest strategist of history, plant her flag and her cannon on Gibraltar, at Quebec, in the Bermudas, at Vancouver, everywhere.
>
> So Hawaii furnishes us a naval base in the heart of the Pacific; the Ladrones another, a voyage further on; Manila another, at the gates of Asia—Asia, to the trade of whose hundreds of millions American merchants, manufacturers, farmers, have as good right as those of Germany or France or Russia or England; Asia, whose commerce with the United Kingdom alone amounts to hundreds of millions of dollars every year; Asia, to whom Germany looks to take her surplus products; Asia, whose doors must not be shut against American trade. Within five decades the bulk of Oriental commerce will be ours.

Having appealed to pride of race, to tradition, to the instinct for profit, and to chauvinistic nationalism, Beveridge last of all returned to the idea of destiny and the Calvinist concept of divine predetermination:

> Wonderfully has God guided us. Yonder at Bunker Hill and Yorktown His providence was above us. At New Orleans and on ensanguined seas His hand sustained us. Abraham Lincoln was His minister and His was the altar of freedom the Nation's soldiers set up on a hundred battle-fields. His power directed Dewey in the East and delivered the Spanish fleet into our hands, as He delivered the elder Armada into the hands of our English sires three centuries ago. . . . We can not fly from our world duties; it is ours to execute the purpose of a fate that has driven us to be greater than our small intentions. We can not retreat from any soil where Providence has unfurled our banner; it is ours to save that soil for liberty and civilization.

There were, of course, voices on the other side. William Jennings Bryan vigorously opposed annexation of the Philippines. Cleveland, who had practically resigned from the Democratic party when Bryan was nominated, joined with him. So did many others who had not sided with Bryan in 1896, among them industrialist Andrew Carnegie and the veteran leader of the reform wing of the Republican party, German-born Carl Schurz. At about the time that Beveridge first delivered his "March of the Flag" speech, Schurz was writing in *Century Magazine* that the mission of America was not to expand but to cultivate its own garden and set an example for the world:

> . . . it is the first and highest duty of the American people, involving their first and gravest responsibility, so to conduct their foreign as well as their domestic concerns that the problem of democratic government on a large scale be successfully solved in this republic, not only for the benefit of the inhabitants of this country alone, but for the benefit of mankind.

Schurz pointed out that democracy was still something new in the world. Most political philosophers in Europe still held that government by an elite, a monarchy or an aristocracy, was better. Democracies, they said, were led by the passions of the mob rather than the cool wisdom of the few. Schurz contended that the paramount duty of Americans was to prove that this was not so. The war with Spain had been, he said, "simply a war of liberation, of humanity, undertaken without any selfish motive." Although he had himself opposed war, he observed:

> If a republican nation can undertake any war without injury to the prestige of democracy as an agency of peace, it is such a war of disinterested benevolence.
>
> But how if this war of humanity and disinterested benevolence be turned into a war of conquest? How if Cuba or any other of the conquered islands be kept by the United States as a permanent possession? . . . how will that cause of civilization fare which consists in the credit of democratic institutions, of the government of, by, and for the people, for which the American people are above all things responsible, and the maintenance of which is above all things their duty and mission? Will not those appear right who say that democratic government is not only no guarantee of peace, but that it is capable of the worst kind of war, the war of conquest, and of resorting to that kind of war, too, as a hypocrite and false pretender?

Like Beveridge, Schurz coupled practical considerations with moral arguments. He did not take issue with Beveridge's assumption that the race to which Americans belonged was superior. But, referring to the facts that 8 to 10 percent of the population was Negro and that each year saw more and more immigration from Latin and Slavic countries, he warned that the people should think less about extending themselves than about protecting what they had:

> We are vexed by a very troublesome race problem in the United States now. That race problem is still unsolved, and it would be very sanguine to say that there is a satisfactory solution in near prospect. Cool-headed men think that we have enough of that. What will be the consequence if we indefinitely add to it by bringing under this republican

government big lots of other incompatible races—races far more intractable, too, than those with which we have had so far to deal?

The people of the Spanish colonies, Schurz also pointed out, were mostly Roman Catholic. If they were taken into the union, even as citizens of territories, the United States might lose its Protestant character. The country could find itself with "millions of people who all belong to one church, and who, if they become a political force, may cause conflicts of influence from which the American people have so far been happily exempt."

Imperialism, Schurz warned, could cause the nation to lose not only its reputation and its racial and religious purity but even the political principles that imperialists talked of spreading to the rest of the globe:

> The admission as States of the Philippines, the Carolines, and so on,—that is, the transformation of "the United States of America" into "the United States of America and Asia,"—would, I suppose, appear too monstrous to be seriously thought of even by the wildest imperialist. Those countries, with an aggregate of about ten million inhabitants, would have to be governed as subject provinces, with no expectation of their becoming self-governing States. This means government without the consent of the governed. It means taxation without representation. It means the very things against which the Declaration of Independence remonstrated, and against which the fathers rose in revolution. It means that the American people would carry on over large subject populations a kind of rule against which their own government is the most solemn protest.

Schurz, like other anti-imperialists, pleaded for preserving the tradition of the Farewell Address. He concluded his article:

> The moral instinct and sound sense of the American people . . . [should] resist . . . the complete abandonment of the principles laid down by George Washington in

From *The Brooklyn Daily "Eagle," January,* 1900.

An anti-expansion cartoonist protests against Uncle Sam's following the counsels of
Senator Beveridge.

his Farewell Address, under the observance of which our
country has grown so prosperous and powerful, and the sub-
stitution therefor of a policy of conquest and adventure—a
policy bound to tarnish our national honor at the first step,
to frighten our American neighbors and to make enemies of
them, to entangle us unnecessarily in the broils of foreign
ambitions, to hazard our peace, to load down our people
with incalculable burdens, to demoralize, deprave, and un-
dermine our democratic government, and thus to unfit the
great American republic for its true mission in the world.

Throughout the summer and early autumn of 1898, arguments echoed through the country. Many shared Schurz's views.
Many more, it seemed, shared Beveridge's. Military and naval
men pointed to the advantages of having a secure, self-sustain-
ing fleet base in the Far East. Business leaders spoke out for
keeping the Philippines so that the United States could pene-
trate the vast and little-developed Asian market. Clergymen

preached on the opportunities for missionary work not only in the Philippines but in the whole Orient. Some went so far as to say that God had given America the Philippines and that it would be sinful to refuse them.

Always a cautious man, McKinley waited to see whether these feelings would last. After receiving the surrender of Spanish forces in Cuba, he had agreed to an armistice. At the time, he insisted on evacuation of Cuba and cession to the United States of Puerto Rico, but he left the Philippine question up in the air. Even when he sent commissioners to Paris to meet with the Spaniards and negotiate a formal peace treaty, he still withheld a decision. Only after touring the Midwest and taking his own soundings of public sentiment did he instruct the commissioners to demand cession of the Philippines.

Although the Spaniards protested, pointing out that American forces had captured only a tiny part of the archipelago, they eventually gave in. The treaty, signed in November, 1898, ceded all the Philippine Islands to the United States.

Those who agreed with Schurz now had only one hope of preventing annexation. No treaty could be ratified until two thirds of the Senate gave its approval. It was possible that more than one third might refuse.

But to the astonishment of nearly everyone, Bryan declared that he would not advise Democratic Senators to vote against ratification. He reasoned that if the treaty did not go through, the war might start up again. Moreover, he conceded that a majority of Senators favored annexation. As a thoroughgoing believer in democracy, he felt that a minority ought not to obstruct the majority. Privately, he may also have wanted the treaty to pass so that he could make it an issue in the 1900 presidential election. In any case, he discouraged all-out battle. Perhaps because of this, the treaty squeaked through by a margin of one vote. The United States thus accepted sovereignty over a colony five thousand miles from its shores.

The debate was far from over. Just before the treaty was ratified, Filipinos demanding independence opened war on the

American occupation troops in the islands. Bloody fighting ensued. Meanwhile, men sympathizing with Schurz organized an Anti-Imperialist League with headquarters in Boston. Pointing to the Philippine insurrection, its members called for granting independence to the islands. They also attacked each suggestion of a new step toward an imperial policy. Sending out speakers and publishing leaflets by the thousands, they kept their viewpoint before the public.

How fervent were the feelings of these anti-imperialists is suggested by the poem "Invocation," written by William Lloyd Garrison, the son of the great abolitionist:

If death be but the open door to light,
The entrance to a kingdom of the soul,
Where eyes from mount of vision may control
The outgrown world with a diviner sight,
O ye, who held the van in freedom's fight,
Reveal to us this troubled nation's goal!
Not more asunder north from southern pole
Than this dark present from your forecast bright.
When the great charter signed by Lincoln's pen
From out the land of bondage brought a race,
How little did ye dream that later men
Would dare this seal of promise to efface!
Has virtue vigor to uprise again,
Or sinks one more republic in disgrace?

In 1900, when Bryan was again nominated by the Democrats to run against McKinley, he saw to it that his platform stressed the Philippine issue. He campaigned as, above all, anti-imperialist.

McKinley would not meet him on this ground. The Republican platform emphasized the country's economic recovery. (Despite the fears of businessmen, the war had helped rather than hurt the business revival.) McKinley's slogan was the "full dinner pail."

McKinley won the election by a larger margin than he had in 1896. Not everyone who voted for him endorsed imperialism. Many who sympathized with Bryan's stand on the

Philippine issue voted against him because they disagreed with his views on free coinage of silver. In many places local issues transcended both the Philippines and free silver. Nevertheless, the electorate clearly did not take a stand against imperialism.

Mahan and others maintained a constant pressure for further territorial extensions. In magazine articles eventually collected in *The Problem of Asia*, the captain argued that it was important for the United States to prevent tsarist Russia or any other nation from becoming dominant in China, even if that meant acquiring stations or colonies on the Asian mainland. In other articles he advocated the building of a canal through Central America and the acquisition of islands and naval bases throughout the Caribbean. Asia, he said, would one day be the world's greatest market. Once an interoceanic canal existed, immense trade would pass through it. The Caribbean would become what historically the Mediterranean had been— the principal highway for commerce between Europe and Asia. The United States ought to ensure, he contended, that this highway was under its exclusive control.

Even before the election of 1900 the McKinley administration showed some disposition to follow Mahan's recommendations. In 1899 Secretary of State John Hay issued the first of the so-called Open Door notes. There seemed then to be danger that Germany, Britain, France, and Russia might partition China as they had partitioned Africa. While Hay did not openly oppose such partitioning, he proposed in this first note that the European powers promise not to curtail trade. Specifically, he asked that, if they did convert parts of China into colonies, they not put tariff barriers around them or discriminate in any way against imports from and exports to other nations.

In 1900, while the presidential campaign was beginning, the antiforeign Boxer uprising took place in China. Foreign diplomats in Peking were besieged and cut off, and all the powers arranged jointly to send troops to their rescue. Hay took the occasion to issue a second Open Door note. In it he declared flatly that the United States stood for the maintenance of China's territorial and administrative integrity. Although addressed as much to the other powers as to Russia, this second note more or less followed Mahan's prescription. The United States did not acquire new colonies as a result of the Open Door notes, but it did assert a direct interest in what happened to China; it warned, in effect, that it might be willing to fight to prevent other nations from dominating that country. At least faintly, the Open Door notes reflected an imperial policy.

In the Caribbean the McKinley administration moved cautiously toward actually taking new territory. Congress debated purchasing or leasing a zone for an interoceanic canal. The State Department negotiated a treaty with Denmark for the purchase of the Danish-owned Virgin Islands. Congress was slow in finishing its work, largely because of differences of opinion on whether the canal should run through Nicaragua or Panama. And, though the United States Senate ratified the treaty with Denmark, the Danish parliament refused its consent. (The islands became American as a result of a new agreement reached in 1917.) But both the legislative and executive branches of the American government were evidently willing to proceed at least a few steps farther along the path of imperialism.

Then, in September, 1901, McKinley was assassinated. Theodore Roosevelt became President. Since Lodge was by now a powerful figure in the Senate, it seemed as if the imperialists were completely in the saddle.

Roosevelt introduced new energy into the conduct of foreign relations. After he took office, Congress at last decided on Panama as the most desirable location for a canal. Since Panama was then a province of Colombia, Roosevelt negotiated a treaty with the Colombian government providing for perpetual lease to the United States of a ten-mile-wide strip across the isthmus. When the Colombian legislature refused to ratify this treaty, Roosevelt tacitly encouraged the Panamanians to revolt and establish an independent republic. Under an American-Colombian agreement dating back to the 1840's, the United States had the right to use force in Panama in order to prevent interruption of transit from one ocean to the other. In the past, American warships and marines had helped Colombia put down uprisings. Now, when the Panamanians revolted, Roosevelt invoked this agreement in their behalf. American warships prevented Colombia from sending in troops to put down the rebellion. Roosevelt meanwhile recognized Panama as independent and negotiated with it a treaty giving the United States a canal zone.

At about the same time, Roosevelt forced a settlement of a long-standing dispute about the boundary between Alaska and Canada. Both the United States and Canada claimed a coastal strip running southeast from Alaska proper. Roosevelt arranged for creation of a six-man commission to decide the issue. The members were supposed to be "impartial jurists of high repute." Roosevelt's three appointees, however, were men fully committed to the American case. (One was Lodge.) And, to make reassurance doubly sure, Roosevelt sent word to London that, even if the commission ruled in favor of Canada, he would occupy the disputed zone with troops. Under this threat, the British member of the commission voted with the three Americans, and the strip became the property of the United States.

But, surprisingly, these were the only steps by Roosevelt that could be classified as clearly imperialistic. He was urged to proceed toward annexation of other islands and base sites in the Caribbean, not only by Mahan and other such writers but also by sources within the government. But he rejected all such advice. The most that he did was to proclaim a "Roosevelt Corollary" to the Monroe Doctrine.

The background of this corollary is complex. For a long time the republic of Venezuela had been a cause of trouble. Its dictator, Cipriano Castro, had mistreated foreign nationals and refused payment on debts to foreign creditors. In 1902, with Roosevelt's consent, the British and German governments exerted pressure on Castro by sending warships to the Venezuelan coast. Public opinion in the United States had, however, reacted unfavorably, interpreting the Anglo-German action as a violation of the Monroe Doctrine. The clamor in the newspapers and in Congress was such that Roosevelt felt compelled to ask the two European powers to withdraw their ships and submit their disputes with Venezuela to arbitration. Soon afterward, when the Dominican Republic was in default on foreign obligations, there was talk once again of punitive action by European states. To prevent a repetition of what had happened in the Venezuelan case, Roosevelt framed his corollary.

The Monroe Doctrine, he said, forbade European powers to take military action against states in the Western Hemisphere; it ought not, however, to give American republics a license to disregard ordinary proprieties. Therefore, he went on, the Doctrine implied a corollary: the United States had a duty to act in the Western Hemisphere as a policeman. If an American republic behaved badly toward a European nation, the United States would punish it or in some way compel it to live up to its obligations. Acting at once under this policy, he arranged for American commissioners to take over customs receipts in the Dominican Republic to pay off European creditors.

Like the Open Door notes, the Roosevelt Corollary had some imperialistic overtones. It claimed for the United States a protective relationship toward all Latin-American nations. At the same time, however, it was a compromise with imperialism. Roosevelt considered intervening forcibly in Venezuela. He was urged to take possession of Santo Domingo, the capital of the Dominican Republic. But he rejected these alternatives in favor of issuing a mere warning to all concerned. Afterward, moreover, he made little or no use of the police power he claimed. When trouble developed in Central America in 1906, he was careful to let Mexico rather than the United States take the lead in developing a solution. His Secretary of State worked meanwhile to promote closer inter-American cooperation. In the later years of his administration, Roosevelt rejected opportunities to annex new territory. Rather than seize new responsibilities, he turned away from them. His policy in the Caribbean was almost the reverse of imperialistic.

In the Far East the same was true. When Roosevelt became President, the danger of Russia's expanding into Manchuria and North China had seemed greater than ever. The British and Japanese were her principal opponents and, owing to the Open Door Policy, the United States was more or less aligned with them. (The Russians thought then, and think now, that there was a secret alliance among the three.) Then, late in 1904, Japan and Russia went to war. To the surprise of most Westerners, the Japanese scored a string of successes. By 1905 both powers were ready for peace (the Japanese because they were fast running out of money). Both hinted in Washington that they would be agreeable to American mediation. Roosevelt, acting on these hints, arranged for a peace conference to meet at Portsmouth, New Hampshire. When the negotiators there reached a deadlock, he stepped in, recommended compromises, and helped them conclude a treaty. Some of Roosevelt's activity seemed a continuation of the quasi-imperial policy symbolized by the Open Door notes—that is, the American government was asserting a strong interest in the Far Eastern balance of power. But in actuality Roosevelt was pulling back from the commitments that had been implied by the Open Door policy. He told friends that he hoped Russia and Japan would offset one another, each preventing the other from expanding at the expense of China. The objectives of the Open Door notes would thus be achieved: China would remain independent and open to foreign trade. But the United States would be able to back out of its role in Asian politics.

While the Russo-Japanese War was still in progress, moreover, Roosevelt held some candid discussions with the Japanese. In Washington he talked with Baron Kentaro Kaneko, an unofficial representative of the Japanese cabinet. Visiting Tokyo, his Secretary of War, William Howard Taft, spoke with the Japanese Foreign Minister, Count Taro Katsura. In return for assurances that Japan would not attempt to take the Philippines from the United States, Roosevelt and Taft agreed to Japan's taking over the independent kingdom of Korea. Later, in a formal agreement, Roosevelt tacitly recognized that Japan was entitled to special consideration in Manchuria. This was hardly protecting the "territorial integrity" of China!

Relations with Japan were not wholly tranquil. Anti-Japanese agitation in California resulted in discrimination against Japanese nationals. Angry reactions in Japan produced a semi-crisis, which was quieted only when Roosevelt transferred the American battle fleet to the Pacific (ostensibly as part of a round-the-world good-will cruise). But it was not the American commitment to the Open Door and the territorial integrity of China that produced the trouble.

In the aftermath of the Spanish war, there had seemed some chance that the United States might play a bigger role in European politics. A number of European statesmen had thought so. In London and Berlin there had been high-level consideration of alliance overtures. The German government never got beyond discussing the possibility, but the British government decided to settle all outstanding disputes with the United States and thus lay the groundwork for future cooperation. By 1905 an incoming Foreign Secretary could declare the preservation of Anglo-American friendship to be one of the three cardinal objectives of British foreign policy. Roosevelt clearly had an opportunity to pursue a more ambitious policy in Europe, but he rejected it.

The turning point was the Moroccan crisis of 1905. The British and French had established an entente (or understanding), one of the bases for which was a mutual agreement that the French should dominate Morocco. The Germans suddenly challenged France's position in that African sultanate. The British backed the French, and it seemed as if the dispute might lead to war. At the request of the German government, Roosevelt acted as an intermediary, helping to arrange a multipower conference at Algeciras, Morocco. American delegates took part in the conference, and its result was to calm the crisis. But, throughout, Roosevelt refused to take sides. Moreover, he warned Europeans that in the future his government would probably not be willing to act even as an honest broker. Convinced, European statesmen stopped thinking of the United States as a possible factor in the European balance of power.

In the Western Hemisphere, American policy at the end of Roosevelt's administration was, in general, to obtain the co-operation of the independent Latin-American republics. In the Far East and Europe the nation's policy was that of the Farewell Address—"to have . . . as little *political* connection as possible." Roosevelt's successors, Taft and Woodrow Wilson, did not materially alter these policies. After having seemed to adopt the imperialist creed of Beveridge and his like, the United States in practice reverted to isolationism.

Why this was so is an intriguing question. Soviet historians call the United States the great capitalist-imperialist nation. They have to explain why the country, after taking the Philippines, failed to gather in other colonies. Their explanation has two parts. In the first place, they charge that Americans practiced economic imperialism: American companies and financial syndicates acquired control of other countries, especially in the Western Hemisphere, and ruled them through native puppet governments; the United States thus added colonies without seeming to. In the second place, they allege that the American government was actually playing a cunning game: while itself standing aloof, it egged other powers into war, intending to wait, jackal-like, until they had cut one another up and the United States would be able to dominate them all. (The basic Soviet text on American diplomatic history, published in 1962, describes the bankruptcy of Europe after World War II as the culmination of this long-laid Wall Street plot.)

American historians have not been so ingenious. Charles A. Beard, author of the famous *Economic Interpretation of the Constitution*, was a scholar prone to explaining events as results of sinister conspiracies on the part of those who stood to make money from them. Although he was no slavish Marxist-Leninist, he was likely in any given case to come up with a Marxist interpretation. Yet when he examined the imperialism of 1898 and after, he had to confess that what had happened was not explicable in economic terms. Writing in *The Idea of National Interest* about the acquisition of Hawaii and the Philippines, he comments:

> . . . there can be no doubt that a sense of moral responsibility was an active factor in bringing about the annexation of new territorial possessions and the efforts to improve the material and spiritual condition of the inhabitants. . . . It was a potent force throughout the country, among millions of American citizens who knew little or nothing about the Philippine Islands, who had no practical interests at stake in their retention or emancipation, who had little information about the possibilities of profit from the development of their natural resources or from the use of them as a base for the enlargement of the China trade. . . .

Practically every American scholar who has studied the record has come to the same conclusion—that the taking of these new territories was a result of a temporary emotional upswell among the public. Each scholar therefore explains the subsequent retreat to isolationism as, in effect, a return to normality. In his *Diplomatic History of the United States*, the dean of American diplomatic historians, Samuel F. Bemis, writes:

> The American people entered into the war with Spain without counting in advance the costs in men and treasure, and they made peace with little heed to the commitments it involved or the possibility of further wars and expenditures much greater in size, which those commitments might bring in another generation. . . . Looking back on those years of adolescent irresponsibility we can now see the acquisition of the Philippines, the climax of American expansion, as a great national aberration.

Without making such explicit condemnation of imperialism, Richard W. Leopold, the author of *The Growth of*

American Foreign Policy, the best recent survey, makes substantially the same appraisal. Describing the roots of imperialism as strategic, economic, religious, and emotional, he comments, "In retrospect, the emotional root appears the most significant. Indeed, it may be argued that the American people quickly turned away from overseas dependencies because once their emotional needs were satisfied, the other pressures were too weak to uphold a policy that did not accord with their traditional ideals or the principles upon which their institutions rested."

Political isolation was the normal condition of the United States. There had simply been a departure from this norm in 1898–1899. But after 1914 there was to be another such aberration. The country was to become involved in a great European war, and after that war the people were to debate earnestly another alternative to isolationism—not imperialism, but internationalism.

Going into World War I

Seventeen years, almost to the day, after the *Olympia* sailed into Manila Bay, another ship, this a passenger liner, weighed anchor for a fateful voyage. The *Lusitania*, pride of the Cunard Company, departed New York for Liverpool, carrying 1,959 passengers and crew, of whom most were English or European but 159 were American.

Across the ocean a great war was going on. Since the summer of 1914, the Allies, Britain, France, and Russia, had been battling the Central Powers, Germany and Austria-Hungary. On land, where lines of trenches and cannon confronted one another, the fighting was ferocious and bloody. Owing to the great superiority of the British navy, there was little fighting at sea. Except on rare occasions, the only German warships that sallied forth were submarines, newly-developed vessels with which the Germans were attacking merchant ships sailing to and from the British Isles. At the insistence of the President of the United States, the German government had promised to conduct submarine operations according to the traditional rules of naval warfare. Presumably, this meant not only that submarines would spare neutral ships but also that they would not torpedo passenger vessels without first surfacing, giving warning, and allowing time for the people aboard, some of whom might be neutrals, to take to lifeboats. Doubting that the Germans

33

would actually keep this promise, the British Admiralty advised liner captains to sail at high speed and follow a zigzag course. But Captain William Turner of the *Lusitania* took it for granted that his giant ship would be safe. Even when entering the submarine-infested Irish Sea, he kept to a steady eighteen knots and steered his usual course.

At 2:10 on the afternoon of May 7, 1915, a torpedo suddenly sliced through the hull starboard side aft. One of those aboard, Charles Lauriat, a Boston book dealer, described what followed:

> Where I stood on deck the shock of the impact was not severe; it was a heavy, rather muffled sound, but the good ship trembled for a moment under the force of the blow; a second explosion quickly followed, but I do not think it was a second torpedo, for the sound was quite different; it was more likely a boiler in the engine room.
>
> As I turned to look in the direction of the explosion I saw a shower of coal and steam and some debris hurled into the air between the second and third funnels, and then heard the fall of gratings and other wreckage that had been blown up by the explosion.

In less than twenty minutes the vessel sank. With her 1,198 people went down, of whom 124 were Americans.

The shock felt in the United States may be hard for later generations to understand. In 1915 war was not yet so all-encompassing as it was to be afterward. A great deal of thought, effort, and emotion had gone into codifying its rules. Not only were neutrals supposed to be left alone, but only in extraordinary circumstances were civilians to be endangered. When attacking France in 1914, the Germans had marched through Belgium. That they did so in disregard of a treaty guaranteeing Belgian neutrality created dismay, and that they then destroyed some churches and university buildings and executed some Belgian civilians intensified it. Even though some of the alleged German atrocities turned out to have been exaggerated or even invented by Allied propagandists, American opinion turned ten to one against Germany. Now that the Germans seemed to

have flouted the laws of sea warfare, many Americans felt that
they had gone beyond the pale.

The same William Lloyd Garrison who had written verse
against imperialism published a poem on the *Lusitania* sinking,
expressing hope that it would not mean war between the United
States and Germany but still voicing the opinion that it had
been an unspeakable and almost intolerable act:

> Avert Thy gaze, O God, close tight Thine eyes!
> Glance down no longer on the ocean foam,
> Lest Thou behold such horrors as can turn
> Men's burning hearts to ice, and chill their souls. . . .
>
> Restrain Thy wrath, and keep Thine hand in check;
> Smite not, nor fiercely thrust without the pale
> Those who can dare to strew the ocean waste
> With fellow creatures, innocent of wrong.
>
> Forget the studied purpose to destroy;
> The launching of the missile through the deep;
> The shattered hull; the crushed and bleeding forms;
> The seething swirl of wreckage, women, men.
>
> Remember that they know not what they do
> Who strike in deadly fear and ghastly hate;
> Remember that somehow, and at some time,
> Each crime exacts its human penalty. . . .

Since President Wilson had warned that, if submarines
did not obey international law, he would hold Germany to
"strict accountability," many people assumed that he would
now take strong measures, perhaps even asking Congress for a
declaration of war. Some wanted him to do so. Theodore Roosevelt issued a statement to the press:

> Centuries have passed since any war vessel of a civi-
> lized power has shown such ruthless brutality toward non-
> combatants, and especially toward women and children. The
> Moslem pirates of the Barbary Coast behaved at times in
> similar fashion, until the civilized nations joined in sup-
> pressing them; and the other pirates who were outcasts from
> among these civilized nations also at one time perpetrated
> similar deeds, until they were sunk or hung. But none of

these old-time pirates committed murder on so vast a scale as in the case of the *Lusitania*. . . .

When those who guide the military policy of a state hold up to the soldiers of their army the Huns, and the terror once caused by the Huns, for their imitation, they thereby render themselves responsible for any Hunnish deed which may follow. The destruction of cities . . . , the scientific vivisection of Belgium as a warning to other nations, the hideous wrongdoing to civilians, men, women and children in Belgium and northern France, in order thereby to terrorize the civilian population—all these deeds, and those like them, done on the land, have now been paralleled by what has happened on the sea.

In the teeth of these things, we earn as a nation measureless scorn and contempt if we follow the lead of those who exalt peace above righteousness, if we heed the voices of those feeble folk who bleat to high heaven that there is peace when there is no peace. For many months our government has preserved between right and wrong a neutrality which would have excited the emulous admiration of Pontius Pilate—the arch-typical neutral of all time. . . .

Unless we act with immediate decision and vigor we shall have failed in the duty demanded by humanity at large, and demanded even more clearly by the self-respect of the American Republic.

Wilson's feelings were more like the poet Garrison's. He shut himself up in the White House until his own emotions and those of the public could cool. Finally, on May 13, he sent to Berlin a strongly worded diplomatic note asking that Germany declare the sinking to have been contrary to her policy, apologize for it, pay conscience money to the bereaved, and repeat her promise to keep submarines within the law. The Germans failed to do these things, replying, indeed, that there had been some justification for the sinking. The *Lusitania*, they said, had carried a cargo of munitions, and its captain had had instructions from the Admiralty to ram a submarine if one surfaced to challenge him. But Wilson still did not act as Roosevelt would have wished. Instead he sent off a second note, declining to debate the case but merely restating his demands.

Even this was too much for some Americans whose views were by now the diametric opposite of Roosevelt's. William Jennings Bryan, the thrice-unsuccessful Democratic candidate for the Presidency, was Wilson's Secretary of State. Feeling deeply, as others did, that no controversy over legal right ought to embroil the United States in a European war, Bryan begged Wilson not to send the second note. Instead he urged Wilson to tell Germany that he would insist on arbitration after the fighting was over and, in order to prevent other incidents, to decree that American citizens must stay off belligerent ships. He wrote the President:

> I beg to renew the suggestions most urgently believing as I do, that without them the note as you outlined it at cabinet meeting would be likely to cause a rupture of diplomatic relations and this might rush us into war in spite of anything we could do. If the initiative were with us I would not fear war, for I am sure you do not want it, but when the note is sent it is Germany's next move—if the note causes her to act in an unfriendly way it may cause conditions here that will increase the difficulties of our position. This may be our last chance to speak for peace, for it will be much harder to propose investigation after some unfriendly act than *now*.
>
> Pardon me for presenting these suggestions so earnestly but I am sure that the sober judgment of the people will not sustain any word or act that provokes war—they will support you if war comes but they will do all in their power to prevent war, and I fully share their desire and purpose in this respect.

When Wilson went ahead with the note, Bryan resigned.

War did not come, at least not immediately. Although the Germans still refused to say that they would do as Wilson asked, in practice they kept submarines in check. In the autumn of 1915 a crisis arose over the sinking of another British passenger liner, the *Arabic*, but the German government declared this to have been a mistake and apologized. In the spring of 1916 another crisis came with the torpedoing of the Channel steamer *Sussex*. This time Wilson delivered an ultimatum, threatening to break diplomatic relations. Again, however, the Germans made amends, now declaring explicitly that submarine captains would, at least in the immediate future, adhere to the traditional rules of international law.

Despite these diplomatic triumphs, the President was under continuous attack at home. On the one hand, Roosevelt's supporters denounced Wilson for failing to go further. On the other, Bryan and his following reproached the President for going as far as he had. Being Democrats, the latter supported him when he was renominated in 1916, but the slogan they used was "He kept us out of war." Wilson himself insisted that he had only kept peace "with honor," implying that he would not necessarily keep it if "honor" were at stake. Accepting the nomination, he summarized his middle-of-the-road position:

We have been neutral not only because it was the fixed and traditional policy of the United States to stand aloof from the politics of Europe and because we had had no part either of action or of policy in the influences which brought on the present war, but also because it was manifestly our duty to prevent, if it were possible, the indefinite extension of the fires of hate and desolation kindled by that terrible conflict and seek to serve mankind by reserving our strength and our resources for the anxious and difficult days of restoration and healing which must follow, when peace will have to build its house anew.

The rights of our own citizens of course became involved: that was inevitable. Where they did this was our guiding principle: that property rights can be vindicated by claims for damages when the war is over, and no modern nation can decline to arbitrate such claims; but the fundamental rights of humanity cannot be. The loss of life is irreparable. Neither can direct violations of a nation's sovereignty await vindication in suits for damages. The nation that violates these essential rights must expect to be checked and called to account by direct challenge and resistance. It at once makes the quarrel in part our own. These are plain principles and we have never lost sight of them or departed from them, whatever the stress or the perplexity of circumstance or the provocation to hasty resentment.

The crucial test for Wilson's policy came in 1917. Concluding that their best chance of winning the war lay in an all-out attempt to cut off Britain's imports of food, the Germans removed all restrictions from submarine commanders. They did so, expecting the United States to go to war but hoping to beat the Allies before Americans were ready to fight effectively. Although Wilson severed diplomatic relations, as he had threatened earlier, he held off temporarily from any more drastic step. Using every means at his command, he pleaded with Germany to change her mind. She did not do so. The unrestricted submarine campaign began on the first of February, and by March not only passenger liners but also American cargo vessels were being torpedoed. Meanwhile, interception of a message from German Foreign Minister Arthur Zimmermann to Mexican President Venustiano Carranza led to discovery that the Germans were seeking an alliance with Mexico, promising restoration to the Mexicans of California, Arizona, and New Mexico.

Many besides those who had backed Roosevelt now felt that the situation called for a declaration of war. Some still fought such a decision. The chairman of the Foreign Relations Committee, William J. Stone of Missouri, spoke out in the Senate. In essence, his arguments were that public opinion was really for peace and that an artificial clamor for war had been stirred up by British propagandists, Americans who were blindly pro-British, and other Americans who were cynically interested in the profits they could make—particularly munitions makers and international bankers. Twenty years later, when the country was again deep in isolationism, many scholars and journalists were to argue exactly these same theses, and their arguments were for a time to be widely accepted. In view of that fact, Stone's speech is worth quoting at length.

Following the custom of the Senate, he addressed his remarks to the presiding officer, the Vice-President, as "Mr. President":

Mr. President, I . . . have here some resolutions some one did me the compliment of transmitting to me by mail, adopted by a gathering of gentlemen who describe themselves as "Sons of the Revolution," demanding that the Congress shall put this country into this war in the name of liberty, and they declare with great vehemence that to stay out of the war would be vile poltroonery and cowardice. I take the liberty of saying that there are "Sons of the Revolution" whose Americanism is distinguished only by the fact that some remote ancestor, lineal or collateral, was indeed a patriot who fought under George Washington against King George for American liberty. There are some such who boast of their lineage, while they forget the lessons of history and treat the admonitions of the fathers with contempt. . . .

No doubt we have "Sons of the Revolution" who regard Washington's admonition as the idle vaporing of an old fogy. But, Mr. President, I hold that Washington's utterance was sound doctrine when he issued his farewell address to his countrymen; issued it not only to his countrymen of his own generation, but to those of the generations that were to follow; and it is sound doctrine now.

Mr. President, we are facing at this time what seems to me to be a very strange situation. A pro-English, anti-German sentiment has grown up in this country, the result of careful and expensive culture, and has taken a form and emphasis which seems to me to be apparently strong enough to endanger our peace with the world. Some German-Americans, so called, and some of their sympathizers, also descended from foreign nationalities, have not been blameless in their attitude and expressions; on the contrary, they have done many things meriting the severest condemnation. But none of them has gone so far in this direction as the pro-English sympathizers, who have thrown off all disguise, and openly declared loyalty to the English cause, and seek with aggressive persistency to force this country into war upon the English side. All this, whether upon the one side or the other, to my thinking is intolerable from the standpoint of true Americanism. I have schooled myself so as to hold myself in hand, that I might stand only to defend and promote the well-being of my own country. I have no hate for Germany; I have no hate for England; I have no hate for any of the peoples engaged in this brutal war. I have even now only one thought or hope to express which might be deemed unneutral, and that is that this war may result in sweeping kings, kaisers, czars, and emperors from power, and that Europe may in the future enjoy the blessings of a real democracy —a democracy that will no longer recognize any divine right of royalty, but will assert the doctrine of the American Declaration of Independence that all men are created equal, and are equal before the law, and that all governmental powers are derived from the people. I would like to see the scions of the House of Hanover, of the Hohenzollerns, the Hapsburgs, and the Romanoffs, with all their progeny, swept from high places of rulership and power. I would like to see that. But during the course of the war I would hold myself aloof from the passion and prejudices of the war. I am free from partisanship. While I pity all who suffer, and would willingly do anything possible that I could honorably do as a neutral friend of all to restore peace to the world, still before everything else my brain, my heart, my soul, are all centered about our America. I am a partisan only of my own country and people. . . .

Mr. President, this is a lawless and brutal war. It is a death grapple. It would seem impossible that either side should win by a fair fight in the open. Each is now struggling to starve the other into submission. Shall we go to the relief of either of them as against the other, or shall we stand aloof, maintaining in good faith our attitude of neutrality, and let them go on to a point when offers of mediation by neutral nations may be received with greater favor than in the past? For myself I would stand aloof. I have no hate for any of these nations; I have pity for all. I am unwilling, with the lights now before me, to plunge my country with a flaming sword into this horror.

Having outlined the horrors of war, Stone then went on to list the groups that he felt would profit from a war. It is here that he most closely anticipated the writers of the 1930's. He said:

Mr. President, who are the instigators of this war propaganda? I can not answer that categorically; but I can answer by asking who would profit by war, and who have vast interests at stake dependent upon the result of the war.

1. I answer, first, that the manufacturers of munitions of war, who so far in supplying foreign demands alone have earned annual dividends running above 250 per cent, would reap an even greater golden harvest if the United States should become involved. Surely they must be behind this war propaganda.

2. The Shipping Trust, headed by the International Mercantile Marine, must be behind it. The International Mercantile Marine was organized by J. P. Morgan & Co., and is currently understood to be partly owned by Mr. Morgan's associates in England. All of you know that now and for a long time trade between the United States and Europe, even neutral Europe, is under the control, regulation, and supervision of Great Britain—Great Britain having arbitrarily taken this control and supervision into the hands of that Government. Without the permission of Great Britain it is hazardous even for a neutral vessel to sail for any European port, and Great Britain assumes to determine what Americans may or may not engage in European export trade. Mr. Morgan's ship company is in no danger of the British blacklist.

3. J. P. Morgan and his associates and syndicates must be behind it. Mr. Morgan is the American fiscal and business agent of the British Government—an enormously profitable employment. It is through him that war loans are made for Great Britain and her allies to the American people, and it is through him that all contracts are made by the British Government with Americans for war supplies. This is a matter of public record, having been so testified to before the Senate Finance Committee. It therefore inevitably follows that the Morgan combination will exhaust all their power to influence public opinion and excite a war spirit in the United States favorable to their employers. Is not that true? And Morgan is reputed to have more control over news agencies than any man in America.

4. American investors in British and other war securities must be behind it. No doubt a thousand million dollars or more of these war securities have been sold in America, chiefly through the Morgan agency. Their value largely depends upon the outcome of the war. Every nation now engaged in this war, whether upon the one side or the other, is staggering upon the verge of national bankruptcy,

and consequently the specter of repudiation is before the eyes of these security holders. At the beginning of this war the President advised American citizens against making investments of this character, and I supplemented this advice of the President in a public statement to the same effect. Of course, both the President and I knew that there was no way under our law to prevent these investments by governmental interdiction; but American citizens were appealed to to keep aloof from such investments, partly because of the risk, and partly on the ground of patriotism, because we knew that whenever an American became financially interested in the success of any one of the belligerents he was apt to become a partisan of that belligerent; and at that time the entire Washington Government was proclaiming the national policy of impartial neutrality. These security holders must be behind this propaganda.

5. In addition to those who have selfish, if not even more sinister, interests at the base of their activities, there are of course a large number of excellent and patriotic people, having no selfish interest to promote, whose undisciplined sympathies have made them partisans in the war, and they therefore are easily excited by the beating of the war drums.

With this latter class I have no quarrel. They have simply lost their balance, and I am sorry. But against munition manufacturers, the Shipping Trust, the Morgan syndicates, and the holders of war securities, who seek to plunge this peaceful and happy Nation into the vortex of war to promote their selfish interests—however they strive to disguise their real purposes by noisy declarations of devoted patriotism—I shall lift my voice in fearless and unflinching protest. The protest may be, probably will be, ineffectual and unavailing, but it will be made.

Lest he be accused of being unpatriotic, Stone concluded:

Mr. President, I want now to speak a word for peace, for "peace hath her victories no less renowned than war." I am not for "peace at any price." I have no sympathy for that sentiment. On the contrary, I believe in maintaining and encouraging the martial spirit in our people. I want them to be willing to fight when the honor and vital interests of the Nation are at stake. I have no regard for the mollycoddle. But I would not inaugurate war for mere aggression, nor inaugurate it until international offense against us makes peace more intolerable than war. I would look with patience upon, and be slow to strike a nation friendly to us not only by tradition, habit, and long years of friendly intercourse, and who did not desire to offend or injure us, and who injures us, if at all, only as an incident to a desperate war with other nations. I would defend the honor and vital interests of my country to the utmost, but I would not have my country going about as a bully with a chip on his shoulder watching for an opportunity to throw all professions of friendship to the winds, and join in a bloody struggle for which we are in nowise responsible and in which our interests are only incidentally involved. . . .

Mr. President, I do not believe the great mass of the American people want the United States to enter this war. I believe they are in sympathy with the views I am expressing. They have approved the past course of the President in keeping us out of this war—this crime of the ages—and I do not believe they have changed their attitude. The opinion of the people on this subject has been too recently and so emphatically expressed for me to believe they have so suddenly changed, even as the wind changes. As late as November last the American electorate, by an unusually large majority, spoke for peace, not war. The jingoes of this country do not speak for the people; the people have just spoken for themselves. Almost on yesterday they reelected Woodrow Wilson to the Presidency, because, above all other reasons, they believed he could not be shaken by jingo clamor or sinister influence of any kind from his firm purpose to employ patiently and resolutely every possible means consistent with the honor and real vital interests of the country to shield his people from actual participation in the horrors of this war. It was that belief and that faith in the President, more than anything else, that brought to him the support of the American people and crowned him afresh with victory. . . .

Wilson finally decided, however, that he had no choice. In early March he had proposed to Congress a measure short of war, the proclamation of an armed neutrality. Guns would be put on American ships, and they would be authorized to shoot submarines on sight, but the United States would not actually join the fighting in Europe. Although the resolution passed the House, it was blocked in the Senate. "A little group of willful men representing no opinion but their own," as Wilson characterized them, filibustered it to death. Wilson meanwhile concluded that, in any case, armed neutrality was not enough. Summoning Congress into joint session, he asked for a declaration of war. Delivering one of the great speeches in American history, he began by summarizing the controversy over submarine warfare:

On the third of February last I officially laid before you the extraordinary announcement of the Imperial German Government that on and after the first day of February it was its purpose to put aside all restraints of law or of humanity and use its submarines to sink every vessel that sought to approach either the ports of Great Britain and Ireland or the western coasts of Europe or any of the ports controlled by the enemies of Germany within the Mediterranean. That had seemed to be the object of the German submarine warfare earlier in the war, but since April of last year the Imperial Government had somewhat restrained the commanders of its undersea craft in conformity with its promise then given to us that passenger boats should not be sunk and that due warning would be given to all other vessels which its submarines might seek to destroy, when no resistance was offered or escape attempted, and care taken that their crews were given at least a fair chance to save their lives in their open boats. The precautions taken were meagre and haphazard enough, as was proved in distressing instance after instance in the progress of the cruel and unmanly business, but a certain degree of restraint was observed. The new policy has swept every restriction aside. Vessels of every kind, whatever their flag, their character, their cargo, their destination, their errand, have been ruthlessly sent to the bottom without warning and without thought of help or mercy for those on board, the vessels of friendly neutrals along with those of belligerents. Even hospital ships and ships carrying relief to the sorely bereaved and stricken people of Belgium, though the latter were provided with safe conduct through the proscribed areas by the German Government itself and were distinguished by unmistakable marks of identity, have been sunk with the same reckless lack of compassion and of principle.

I was for a little while unable to believe that such things would in fact be done by any government that had hitherto subscribed to the humane practices of civilized nations. International law had its origin in the attempt to set up some law which would be respected and observed upon the seas, where no nation had right of dominion and where lay the free highways of the world. By painful stage after stage has that law been built up, with meagre enough results, indeed, after all was accomplished that could be accomplished, but always with a clear view, at least, of what the heart and conscience of mankind demanded. This minimum of right the German Government has swept aside under the plea of retaliation and necessity and because it had no weapons which it could use at sea except these which it is impossible to employ as it is employing them without throwing to the winds all scruples of humanity or of respect for the understandings that were supposed to underlie the intercourse of the world. I am not now thinking of the loss of property, immense and serious as that is, but only of the wanton and wholesale destruction of the lives of non-combatants, men, women, and children, engaged in pursuits which have always, even in the darkest periods of modern history, been deemed innocent and legitimate. Property can be paid for; the lives of peaceful and innocent people cannot be. The present German submarine warfare against commerce is a warfare against mankind.

After this introduction, Wilson began to develop the theme that the purpose of a war against Germany would be more than to punish her for not living up to her promises. Speaking of the German submarine campaign, he went on:

It is a warfare against all nations. American ships have been sunk, American lives taken, in ways which it has stirred us very deeply to learn of, but the ships and the people of other neutral and friendly nations have been sunk and overwhelmed in the waters in the same way. There has been no discrimination. The challenge is to all mankind. Each nation must decide for itself how it will meet it. The choice we make for ourselves must be made with a moderation of counsel and a temperateness of judgment befitting our character and our motives as a nation. We must put excited feeling away. Our motive will not be revenge or the victorious assertion of the physical might of the nation, but only the vindication of right, of human right, of which we are only a single champion. . . .

. . . There is one choice we cannot make, we are incapable of making: we will not choose the path of submission and suffer the most sacred rights of our nation and our people to be ignored or violated. The wrongs against which we now array ourselves are no common wrongs; they cut at the very roots of human life.

With a profound sense of the solemn and even tragical character of the step I am taking and of the grave responsibilities which it involves, but in unhesitating obedience to what I deem my constitutional duty, I advise that the Congress declare the recent course of the Imperial German Government to be in fact nothing less than war against the government and people of the United States; that it formally accept the status of belligerent which has thus been thrust upon it; and that it take immediate steps not only to put the country in a more thorough state of defense but also to exert all its power and employ all its resources to bring the Government of the German Empire to terms and end the war. . . .

. . . Our object . . . is to vindicate the principles of peace and justice in the life of the world as against selfish and autocratic power and to set up amongst the really free and self-governed peoples of the world such a concert of purpose and of action as will henceforth ensure the observance of those principles. Neutrality is no longer feasible or desirable where the peace of the world is involved and the freedom of its peoples, and the menace to that peace and freedom lies in the existence of autocratic governments backed by organized force which is controlled wholly by their will, not by the will of their people. We have seen the last of neutrality in such circumstances. We are at the beginning of an age in which it will be insisted that the same standards of conduct and of responsibility for wrong done shall be observed among nations and their governments that are observed among the individual citizens of civilized states. . . .

Having thus recommended a declaration of war as a matter of moral duty, Wilson spoke of the noble purposes that war might serve. Even before the *Lusitania* incident, he had expressed hope that the United States might have some voice in the ultimate peace settlement. He reasoned that it was so great a power, with so many farflung interests and with such a diverse population, that it could not fail to be touched by any great war anywhere on the globe. That being the case, he felt that it had as much interest as other nations in seeing that no war erupted again. By 1916 he had become convinced that the means to such an end was the establishment of a League of Nations. There all states could have a voice, all issues could be aired, and the might of many could be brought to bear collectively against any one that disrupted the peace. He had said repeatedly that the United States ought to play an important part in such a League. In late 1916 and early 1917, he had appealed to all the belligerents to negotiate a "peace without victory" and join in creating institutions that would guarantee permanent peace in the future. The German response to his appeal had been the announcement of unrestricted submarine warfare.

Now, he told Congress, the German government had to be regarded as an enemy of peace. The German people, he said, shared the hopes and aspirations of people in other lands. But before they could cooperate with the rest of mankind, their autocratic and militaristic government would have to be overthrown as tsarist Russia's had been in the revolution of March, 1917. War would have this object—of removing the obstacle to lasting peace. And beyond that it would have the aim of creating the structure for such a peace. Wilson said to Congress:

> We are accepting [Germany's] challenge of hostile purpose because we know that in such a government . . . we can never have a friend; and that in the presence of its organized power, always lying in wait to accomplish we know not what purpose, there can be no assured security for the democratic governments of the world. We are now about to

accept gauge of battle with this natural foe to liberty and shall, if necessary, spend the whole force of the nation to check and nullify its pretensions and its power. We are glad, now that we see the facts with no veil of false pretence about them, to fight thus for the ultimate peace of the world and for the liberation of its peoples, the German peoples included: for the rights of nations great and small and the privilege of men everywhere to choose their way of life and of obedience. The world must be made safe for democracy. Its peace must be planted upon the tested foundations of political liberty. We have no selfish ends to serve. We desire no conquest, no dominion. We seek no indemnities for ourselves, no material compensation for the sacrifices we shall freely make. We are but one of the champions of the rights of mankind. We shall be satisfied when those rights have been made as secure as the faith and the freedom of nations can make them. . . .

It is a distressing and oppressive duty, Gentlemen of the Congress, which I have performed in thus addressing you. There are, it may be, many months of fiery trial and sacrifice ahead of us. It is a fearful thing to lead this great peaceful people into war, into the most terrible and disastrous of all wars, civilization itself seeming to be in the balance. But the right is more precious than peace, and we shall fight for the things which we have always carried nearest our hearts,—for democracy, for the right of those who submit to authority to have a voice in their own governments, for the rights and liberties of small nations, for a universal dominion of right by such a concert of free peoples as shall bring peace and safety to all nations and make the world itself at last free. To such a task we can dedicate our lives and our fortunes, everything that we are and everything that we have, with the pride of those who know that the day has come when America is privileged to spend her blood and her might for the principles that gave her birth and happiness and the peace which she has treasured. God helping her, she can do no other.

Responding to this appeal, the two houses voted overwhelmingly for war.

Afterward, historians were to debate fiercely about the causes of America's intervention in World War I. From the

late 1920's down to the beginning of World War II, the most
common view among scholars was that Senator Stone had been
essentially correct: British propagandists, abetted by Americans
with a financial stake in Allied victory, had whipped up public
feeling. Influenced by the public mood and misled by pro-Ally
advisers, Wilson became unduly harsh and stubborn in his
stand against submarine warfare. The United States thus threw
itself into war unnecessarily and, in doing so, injured not only
itself but the world, for the world would have been better off
if the Allies and Central Powers had fought to a draw and
arranged a negotiated peace.

This interpretation soon lost popularity. World War II
convinced most Americans that what happened to Europe was
of vital importance for the United States. Looking back to
1917, some persuaded themselves that the nation must have
gone to battle then in order to prevent Germany from con-
quering the continent. When scholars inspected this thesis,
they found little evidence to support it. To be sure, some of
Wilson's close advisers had privately taken the view that the
United States, like Britain in the past, ought to seek the preservation of a balance of power in Europe. Robert Lansing, the
cold, handsome New York lawyer who succeeded Bryan as
Secretary of State, wrote in his diary in 1915 that United States
policy should look forward to "actual participation in the war
in case it becomes evident that Germany will be the victor. . . .
Germany must not be permitted to win . . . or to break
even. . . ."

Wilson, however, never expressed such a view. On the
contrary, he spoke contemptuously of the balance of power as
"forever discredited." Historians reviewing the evidence in the
1950's and 1960's were to find Wilson's decision for war one
that could be explained only tentatively. Arthur Link, author
of the definitive biography of Wilson, summarizes in a long
essay, *Wilson the Diplomatist*, the factors that probably entered the President's thoughts during the crucial days when

he composed his war message. With only shades of difference, most historians would probably agree with this summary:

> One of the most important . . . factors was the subtlest and the one for which the least direct evidence can be adduced. It was Wilson's apparent fear that the threat of a German victory imperiled the balance of power and all his hopes for the future reconstruction of the world community. We must be careful here not to misinterpret his thoughts and motives. There is little evidence that he accepted the decision for war because he thought that a German victory would seriously endanger American security, because he wanted to preserve Anglo-American control of the North Atlantic sea lanes, or because he desired to maintain the traditional balance of European power because it served American interests. Nor is there any convincing evidence that Wilson's attitude toward the objectives of the rival alliances had changed by the time that he made his final decision.
>
> On the other hand, there was now a great and decisive difference in the relative position of the belligerents: The Allies seemed about to lose the war and the Central Powers about to win it. This, almost certainly, was a governing factor in Wilson's willingness to think in terms of war. Germany, he told Colonel House, was a madman who must be curbed. A German victory meant a peace of domination and conquest; it meant the end of all of Wilson's dreams of helping to build a secure future.
>
> As the President pondered America's duty at this juncture in history, the answer must have seemed obvious to him—to accept belligerency, because now only through belligerency could the United States fulfill its mission to insure a just and lasting peace of reconciliation. This could be accomplished only by preventing a German victory and only by the assertion of such power and influence among the Allies as would come to the United States by virtue of its sacrifice of blood and treasure.
>
> If the immediate events made a war resolution necessary, then the goal of a righteous peace was the objective that justified full-scale participation in Wilson's mind and raised that effort to a high and noble plane. . . .

The combined weight of official and public opinion was another pressure meanwhile driving Wilson toward acceptance of the decision for war. It was a fact of no little consequence that by the end of March every important member of the administration, including those members of the Cabinet who had heretofore opposed any bellicose measures, urged the President to admit that a state of war with Germany in fact existed. Public opinion had remained stubbornly pacific until near the end of February, 1917. Then the publication of the Zimmermann telegram, in which the German government proposed to Mexico a war alliance against the United States . . . and, above all, the destruction of American ships in the war zones after mid-March generated a demand for war that grew with mounting crescendo in all sections and among all classes, until it seemed beyond doubt to be a national and a majority demand. It was further stimulated by news of the downfall of the czarist regime and the establishment of a provisional republican government in Russia—news that convinced many wavering Americans that the Allies were indeed fighting for democracy and also changed overnight the large and influential American Jewish community from a position of strong hostility toward the Allies to one of friendship.

This was all a development of profound importance for a leader as keenly sensitive to public opinion as was Woodrow Wilson. He could have joined forces with the large antiwar minority to resist the demand for war; indeed, he probably would have done so had he been convinced that it was the wise and right thing to do. The point is not, therefore, that public opinion *forced* Wilson to accept the decision for war, but that it facilitated doing what Wilson for other reasons now thought was necessary and right to do.

All this is said without any intention of implying that Wilson ever *wanted* war. The agony of his soul was great as he moved through the dark valley of his doubts. He had no illusions about the merits of the conflict into which he and his people were being drawn. He saw the risks of intervention, both to his own nation and to the world, with remarkable clarity. But he could devise no alternative; and he set aside his doubts in the hope that acting now as a belligerent, with all the power and idealism of the American people sustaining him, he could achieve objectives to justify the misery of mankind.

The Struggle
for a
Just Peace

Wilson's war message had indicated that America's intervention in World War I was not just for the purpose of punishing Germany. He stated noble, positive aims. Even earlier, when still expressing hope of staying out of the war, he had said, "We can no longer indulge our traditional provincialism. We are to play a leading part in the world drama whether we wish it or not."

During the war he developed more fully the ideas he had sketched in his war message. The Russian Revolution, which had at first seemed such a hopeful event, had changed its character. In November, 1917, Lenin and the Communists had come to power. Charging that the Americans and the European Allies were no better than the Germans, they called upon workers and peasants in all countries to revolt—to stop fighting for their countries and start fighting against their own governments. Lenin meanwhile opened negotiations with the Germans for a separate peace. Attempting both to answer the Communist charges and to persuade the Russians that they should continue in the war, Wilson on January 4, 1918, made known fourteen points that he considered "the only possible program" for peace. These fell into three general categories. First came suggestions for removing the conditions of war:

53

1. Open covenants of peace, openly arrived at, after which there shall be no private international understandings of any kind but diplomacy shall proceed always frankly and in the public view.

2. Absolute freedom of navigation upon the seas, outside territorial waters, alike in peace and in war, except as the seas may be closed in whole or in part by international action for the enforcement of international covenants.

3. The removal, so far as possible, of all economic barriers and the establishment of an equality of trade conditions among all the nations consenting to the peace and associating themselves for its maintenance.

4. Adequate guarantees given and taken that national armaments will be reduced to the lowest points consistent with domestic safety.

5. A free, open-minded, and absolutely impartial adjustment of all colonial claims, based upon a strict observance of the principle that in determining all such questions of sovereignty the interests of the populations concerned must have equal weight with the equitable claims of the government whose title is to be determined.

Next he listed points of self-determination:

6. The evacuation of all Russian territory and such a settlement of all questions affecting Russia as will secure the best and freest cooperation of the other nations of the world in obtaining for her an unhampered and unembarrassed opportunity for the independent determination of her own political development and national policy and assure her of a sincere welcome into the society of free nations under institutions of her own choosing; and, more than a welcome, assistance also of every kind that she may need and may herself desire. The treatment accorded Russia by her sister nations in the months to come will be the acid test of their good will, of their comprehension of her needs as distinguished from their own interests, and of their intelligent and unselfish sympathy.

7. Belgium, the whole world will agree, must be evacuated and restored, without any attempt to limit the sovereignty which she enjoys in common with all other free nations. No other single act will serve as this will serve to restore confidence among the nations in the laws which they

have themselves set and determined for the government of their relations with one another. Without this healing act the whole structure and validity of international law is forever impaired.

8. All French territory should be freed and the invaded portions restored, and the wrong done to France by Prussia in 1871 in the matter of Alsace-Lorraine, which has unsettled the peace of the world for nearly fifty years, should be righted, in order that peace may once more be made secure in the interest of all.

9. A readjustment of the frontiers of Italy should be effected along clearly recognizable lines of nationality.

10. The peoples of Austria-Hungary, whose place among the nations we wish to see safeguarded and assured, should be accorded the freest opportunity of autonomous development.

11. Rumania, Serbia, and Montenegro should be evacuated; occupied territories restored; Serbia accorded free and secure access to the sea; and the relations of the several Balkan states to one another determined by friendly counsel along historically established lines of allegiance and nationality; and international guarantees of the political and economic independence and territorial integrity of the several Balkan states should be entered into.

12. The Turkish portions of the present Ottoman Empire should be assured a secure sovereignty, but the other nationalities which are now under Turkish rule should be assured an undoubted security of life and an absolutely unmolested opportunity of autonomous development, and the Dardanelles should be permanently opened as a free passage to the ships and commerce of all nations under international guarantees.

13. An independent Polish state should be erected which should include the territories inhabited by indisputably Polish populations, which should be assured a free and secure access to the sea, and whose political and economic independence and territorial integrity should be guaranteed by international covenant.

Finally came his proposal for the League of Nations:

14. A general association of nations must be formed under specific covenants for the purpose of affording mutual

guarantees of political independence and territorial integrity
to great and small states alike.

Adding some generalities to these specific points, Wilson
went on in the same speech to declare:

> In regard to these essential rectifications of wrong
> and assertions of right we feel ourselves to be intimate part-
> ners of all the governments and peoples associated together
> against the imperialists. We cannot be separated in interest
> or divided in purpose. We stand together until the end.
>
> For such arrangements and covenants we are willing
> to fight and to continue to fight until they are achieved; but
> only because we wish the right to prevail and desire a just
> and stable peace such as can be secured only by removing
> the chief provocations to war, which this program does re-
> move.

Wilson asked that Germany *not* be punished:

> We have no jealousy of German greatness, and there
> is nothing in this program that impairs it. We grudge her no
> achievement or distinction of learning or of pacific enterprise
> such as have made her record very bright and very enviable.
> We do not wish to injure her or to block in any way her
> legitimate influence or power. We do not wish to fight her
> either with arms or with hostile arrangements of trade if she
> is willing to associate herself with us and the other peace-
> loving nations of the world in covenants of justice and law
> and fair dealing.
>
> We wish her only to accept a place of equality among
> the peoples of the world,—the new world in which we now
> live,—instead of a place of mastery. . . .
>
> We have spoken now, surely, in terms too concrete
> to admit of any further doubt or question. An evident prin-
> ciple runs through the whole program I have outlined. It is
> the principle of justice to all peoples and nationalities, and
> their right to live on equal terms of liberty and safety with
> one another, whether they be strong or weak.
>
> Unless this principle be made its foundation no part
> of the structure of international justice can stand. . . .

Although Wilson's words had little impact on the Russian leaders, who went ahead and made peace with the Germans, they reached the hearts of millions not only in the Allied countries but also in Germany and Austria-Hungary. In the Fourteen Points these people saw the outlines of a settlement based on justice—one that would eradicate the ancient causes for international antagonism and perhaps enable men thereafter for the first time to live without fear of war.

As the months ground on, the numbers attracted by Wilson's vision increased. By early autumn of 1918 Germany's leaders were aware that their armies had been defeated in the field. A new cabinet took over. In early October it sent a message to Washington by way of Switzerland proposing that peace be made on the basis of the points and principles that Wilson had voiced.

Many people on the Allied side were suspicious of this overture. They feared that the Germans might be playing a trick. Wilson himself was dubious. In responding, he asked for assurances that Germany would really accept his points, not just treat them as subjects for debate. He also emphasized that he would deal only with a German government that truly represented its public.

Growing weaker and weaker, the Germans gave Wilson all the guarantees he asked. While messages were being exchanged, moreover, the German emperor fled his country; a republic was proclaimed; and a Socialist took office as president. Allied statesmen stalled. Wanting territorial and economic gains for their countries, they had reservations about Wilson's points. But, when faced with a threat that the United States might make peace separately, they came around. A pre-armistice agreement signed in Paris in late October committed the chief Allied governments to Wilson's points and to the general principle of treating Germany justly rather than vengefully. Thus, when the armistice itself came on November 11, all parties, victors and vanquished alike, were committed to negotiate a peace based on Wilsonian ideals.

The conference to draw up the peace treaty convened in Paris early in 1919. Establishing a new precedent, Wilson went in person. For the better part of five months, he met face to face with other national leaders, trying to turn his earlier generalities into the hard, precise language of multi-national accords. Despite the pre-armistice agreement, the French premier, Georges Clemenceau, fought tooth and nail for provisions that, whether just or not, would make France stronger than Germany. British Prime Minister David Lloyd George fought similarly for economic advantages and for the enlargement of the British Empire. The Italian delegates were intent on getting new territory for Italy; the Japanese wanted to keep the leaseholds in China that they had taken over from the Germans. The new states of eastern Europe, Poland and Czechoslovakia, wanted to be as large as possible. So did Serbia, which had already expanded (in 1929 renamed Yugoslavia). So did Rumania and Greece, both of which had taken part in the war against Germany and Austria-Hungary. Spokesmen for these nations and for nationality groups elsewhere in Europe, the Middle East, and the Far East were all in Paris, and the clamor of all but a few was for national advantage. Wilson stood almost alone for a peace based on the abstract principle of justice.

At home, meanwhile, his political opponents were busy undermining his strength. In the midterm elections of 1918 the Republican party had won majorities in both houses of Congress. The Republican leader in foreign affairs was Henry Cabot Lodge, now nearly seventy, the prospective chairman of the Senate Foreign Relations Committee. And Lodge hated Wilson. The reason may have been nothing more than that Wilson had robbed him of the title "scholar in politics." In any case, his hatred was passionate and consuming, and he made it his object at every stage to embarrass, weaken, or frustrate the President.

In Paris Wilson chose the tactic of giving priority to the proposed League of Nations. Recognizing that the final treaty would be imperfect at best, he emphasized the importance of establishing a world organization that could hear future grievances, make changes in the treaty's terms, and ensure that, in the long run, peace and justice would prevail. He insisted that, before going on to specific territorial or economic issues, the delegates agree on a charter or Covenant for the League.

Despite opposition from Clemenceau, Lloyd George, and others, Wilson won his point. Agreement was reached on a Covenant. The projected League was to have an Assembly where all nations would be represented and where any and all issues could be aired. It was also to have a Council representing mainly the great powers. In the event that one state should in the future commit aggression or otherwise endanger peace, the Council was to have the duty of mobilizing all other states in collective action. The key provisions were Articles 10 and 11 of the Covenant:

Article 10

The Members of the League undertake to respect and preserve as against external aggression the territorial and existing political independence of all Members of the League. In case of any such aggression or in case of any threat or danger of such aggression the Council shall advise upon the means by which this obligation shall be fulfilled.

Article 11

Any war or threat of war, whether immediately affecting any of the Members of the League or not, is hereby declared a matter of concern to the whole League, and the League shall take any action that may be deemed wise and effectual to safeguard the peace of nations. In case any such emergency should arise the Secretary General shall on the request of any Member of the League forthwith summon a meeting of the Council.

No sooner had the Covenant been drawn up in Paris, however, than Lodge and his cohorts launched an attack on it. The key articles, they warned, were likely to embroil the United States in European disputes and unnecessarily draw the nation into future European wars. They demanded that the

Covenant be amended so that a member of the League would have the right to resign, so that the League would be unable to interfere in tariff, immigration, and other "domestic" matters, and so that the Monroe Doctrine would be preserved intact. Enough Senators joined in these demands to make it clear that the Covenant would not be ratified unless it were changed.

To his chagrin, Wilson had to ask Clemenceau, Lloyd George, and the others to accept amendments that would satisfy some of the senatorial criticism. This opened the floodgates. Asked in return to make concessions on territorial and economic questions, Wilson had little choice but to bend. As terms were developed for treaties with Germany, Austria, Hungary (which had made itself independent), and Turkey, one compromise provision after another went in. Instead of being dealt with evenhandedly, the Germans were made to give up territory in which the population was largely German, to accept military clauses that, if enforced, would make Germany permanently inferior to France, to promise reparations payments of astronomical proportions, and, gallingly, to state that Germany alone had begun the war and was therefore responsible for all the suffering the world had undergone.

Wilson did not lose every battle. He prevented the French from getting all the border territory they wanted. Some of the districts taken from Germany were promised plebiscites so that their people would someday have a chance to vote on whether or not to rejoin their fatherland. Actual reparations payments were to be determined by a Reparations Commission; the United States would presumably have a representative on that commission, and he would be able to exercise a restraining influence on the other members. Italy was denied some of her demands, notably that for the city of Fiume on the Adriatic. Although given control over the former German leasehold in Shantung, the Japanese were obliged to promise that they would eventually restore it to China. Above all, the basic provisions for the League remained intact. The Covenant was to be part of each peace treaty. Wilson could hope that the League could eventually make right whatever wrongs the treaties themselves might perpetrate.

Internationalism
or
Isolationism?

Wilson's hopes may or may not have been realistic. In light of what happened later, after Hitler took over, it has been argued that the peacemakers of 1919 were too easy on the Germans—too concerned with justice and too little with security, power, and the like. But all this is abstract speculation. The League of Nations, as Wilson conceived it, was never to be given a chance.

Opposition to it in the United States had not been stilled by the amendments to the Covenant that Wilson had obtained in Paris. Following Lodge's guidance, Republicans continued to criticize the Covenant, complaining that the United States would be in danger of being drawn into wars that were none of its business; that the League might meddle in Latin-American affairs; and that foreign powers might try to tell the United States what its tariffs and immigration laws should be. Some were sincere. Others were merely partisan, the real ground for their opposition being the fact that Wilson had not consulted members of the opposition party (or even members of the Senate) and that the Covenant seemed the exclusive handiwork of a Democratic President.

But outside the ranks of regular Republicans were many whose objections were genuine. German-Americans had never forgiven Wilson for entering the war. Persecuted by superpatriots, they had grown more and more bitter while the war was on. Now they were violently angry that Wilson had retreated from his promise of justice for their defeated fatherland. Nor were they alone. Some Italian-Americans were outspokenly resentful of Wilson's refusal to give Fiume to Italy, and, in varying degrees, members of other national minority groups were critical of him. Americans who cherished the Open Door tradition felt that the United States should never put its seal of approval on Japan's takeover of Shantung. A surprising number of left-wing Democrats, formerly ardent supporters of Wilson, disapproved of the peace settlement because of the number of compromises that had been made. The treaties were too full of injustices and inequities, they contended, and the League was less likely to remedy them than to enforce their continuation. While surveys of public opinion indicated that the majority supported Wilson, his opponents were numerous and their feelings were intense.

In the Senate, fourteen members, mostly Republicans, styled themselves *irreconcilables*. They held that the treaties and the League Covenant, which was to be part of them, ought not in any circumstances to be ratified. Robert M. LaFollette of Wisconsin, one of them, put his case this way:

We have already paid a fearful price for our participation in the late war. It has cost us the lives of more than 50,000 of our finest young men slain in battle, and over 200,000 maimed and wounded, and many thousands of others who lost their lives through disease growing out of the war. It has cost us some thirty billions of dollars, most of which still remains to be wrung from our people—principal and interest—by heartbreaking taxes which must be paid by this and succeeding generations. . . .

Every Senator when he cast his vote for war knew that it meant the things I have mentioned. This much we contracted for when we entered the war. And, sir, these are the burdens which the mass of people of this country must bear, and a part of which must be passed on to succeeding generations. No one doubts that we are strong enough and resourceful enough to pay in full our war debts; and if we go our way in peace, we will in time be able to restore our country to normal conditions. We can never bring back the lives that were sacrificed; we can never restore the maimed and wounded to health. The hearts broken through this war we can never heal; the suffering it has entailed we can never recall; and all that we knew we bargained for when we entered the war.

But, sir, there is one thing which is now demanded of us that we did not bargain for when we entered this war, and that is the surrender of our right to control our own destiny as a Nation.

After all, Mr. President, that is what membership in this proposed league of nations is to cost us. Up until the present time we are still free to travel the road which the founders of our Government intended us to travel. We are still free to fulfill the destiny for which we are fitted by the genius of our people, the character of our institutions, our great resources, and our fortunate geographical position. All this we are asked to surrender in order to become a member of this league of nations. We are asked to emasculate, if not destroy, our form of government by recognizing the right of some assembly or council of nations, in which we have small voice, to interfere with our most vital concerns. We are asked to place our resources, not only our wealth, but the lives of our people, at the disposal of Governments and peoples in the remote sections of the earth and to uphold there policies foreign to the purposes and desires of our own people. We are asked to depart from the traditional policy which our position on the American Continent has enabled us to pursue of keeping free from entangling alliances of European politics, and to become a party to every political scheme that may be hatched in the capitals of Europe or elsewhere in this world of ours.

This, Mr. President, is something that no one contemplated when we entered the war, and I do not believe that one vote in favor of the war would have been cast in the Congress of the United States if it had been understood that such a result would follow our participation in the war. . . .

Expanding on this theme, LaFollette went on to protest Article 10 of the Covenant. Under it, members of the League would be bound to preserve the territorial integrity and political independence of all other members:

> Now, either we are going to do that, specifically that thing, or we are not going to do it. If we are not going to do it, we have no business in the league. We can not promise to preserve political independence and territorial integrity of some members and not of others. We can not promise to preserve the territorial integrity and political independence of the members of the league on some occasions and refuse to do it on other occasions. We can not be permitted to preserve the political independence and territorial integrity of a member of the league when it is to our interest to do so and seek to destroy the political independence or territorial integrity of a member of the league when it is to our interest to take that course. Such action on the part of the members of the league would destroy the whole plan and purpose of the league. It would at once reduce it to a mere aggregation of warring factions and petty alliances, in which every dispute submitted to the league would beget as many others as there are members of the league. I assume that if we go into the league we go into it with the honest intention of fulfilling our obligation to preserve the political and territorial status quo created by the peace conference at Paris. . . .
>
> No rational man can doubt but the United States will be the Nation relied upon to furnish the men and the money to enforce the decrees and mandates of the league throughout central Europe and parts of Asia and Africa.
>
> Who can doubt that the self-interest of Italy, Roumania, Greece, and Serbia, when they find their ambitions thwarted by the more powerful members of the league, particularly by the United States, will come together in a union of self-interest, and what we start to do in the first instance with a few thousand men we shall soon find requires a vast army? All this and vastly more is involved in the obligations we will assume under article 10 of this treaty.

Nor was it only the prospective sacrifices that worried LaFollette. He was also troubled by the fact that the United

States might be obliged to uphold the injustices the peace treaties had wrought and even fight to keep them in effect. He concluded:

> Mr. President, the little group of men who sat in secret conclave for months at Versailles were not peacemakers. They were war makers. They cut and slashed the map of the Old World in violation of the terms of the armistice. They patched up a new map of the Old World in consummation of the terms of the secret treaties the existence of which they had denied because they feared to expose the sordid aims and purposes for which men were sent to death by the tens of thousands daily. They betrayed China. They locked the chains on the subject peoples of Ireland, Egypt, and India. They partitioned territory and traded off peoples in mockery of that sanctified formula of 14 points, and made it our Nation's shame. Then, fearing the wrath of outraged peoples, knowing that their new map would be torn to rags and tatters by the conflicting warring elements which they had bound together in wanton disregard of racial animosities, they made a league of nations to stand guard over the swag!
> The Old World armies were exhausted. Their treasuries were empty. It was imperative that they should be able to draw upon the lusty man power and the rich material resources of the United States to build a military cordon around the new boundaries of the new States of the Old World.
> Senators, if we go into this thing, it means a great standing Army; it means conscription to fight in foreign wars, a blighting curse upon the family life of every American home, every hour. It means higher taxes, higher prices, harder times for the poor. It means greater discontent; a deeper, more menacing unrest.
> Mr. President, whatever course other Senators take, I shall never vote to bind my country to the monstrous undertaking which this covenant would impose.

The fourteen irreconcilables were, of course, a minority. Although all Republicans were critical of aspects of the treaties, most said they would vote for ratification if certain amendments or reservations were attached. All the Democrats (except two irreconcilables) were prepared to approve the treaties with no changes at all. On the surface, this seemed to make ratification a certainty. But the Constitution requires a two-thirds vote to pass a treaty. In a Senate of ninety-six, the irreconcilables needed only nineteen allies. About half the Republicans were "strong reservationists." They held that important parts of the Covenant or the treaties should be rejected or drastically altered. If their wishes were not satisfied, some might go over to the irreconcilables. On the other hand, if the Republican leadership pressed the tough reservations that this group wanted, the result might be to make the treaties unacceptable to others. Wilson, the Democrats, or even the Republican "mild reservationists" might decide they preferred no treaties at all to ones shorn of adequate provision for collective security. In that case, the warm friends of the Covenant might end up voting with its bitter enemies.

This complex situation was made to order for Lodge. The first and most important treaty, that with Germany, was signed at Versailles in early June, 1919. When presented to the Senate by Wilson, it was referred to Lodge's Foreign Relations Committee. The Massachusetts Senator then made it plain that he would postpone a vote as long as he could. He read the whole 268-page text aloud to the committee. Afterward, he entertained a parade of witnesses, many of whom testified at length about irrelevant matters. Meanwhile, a stream of rumors issued from the committee, hinting at the amendments or reservations it was likely to recommend. In all probability, Lodge inspired these in a deliberate effort to maneuver Wilson into stating publicly which changes he would regard as completely unacceptable. Once Wilson was committed in such fashion, Lodge could then attempt to unite the Republican majority behind those changes. Wilson would then be left with only two alternatives: to surrender, letting the Democrats vote for a ruined treaty; or to mobilize the Democrats against the Republican reservations, block ratification, and thus destroy his own creation. In either event, Lodge's aim would have been achieved, for Wilson would have suffered public humiliation.

Wilson himself was, of course, no mean political tactician. No President except Franklin Roosevelt has had more success in whipping legislators into line. Sensing Lodge's purpose, he avoided committing himself strongly against any particular reservation. Contenting himself with arguing in general terms against any reservations at all, he sought to wait Lodge out. Meanwhile, in privacy, he meditated possible formulae by means of which he could unite the Democrats and the Republican mild reservationists.

Wilson discovered, however, that time worked for Lodge. With the war over, consumer goods returning to store shelves, prices skyrocketing, labor unions going out on strike, lunatics sending bombs through the mails to statesmen and financiers, and Chicago White Sox players conspiring to fix a World Series, the public was losing interest in the League question. By and large, the people who continued intently to follow the debate were those who opposed ratification. Wilson concluded that, if he continued fencing with Lodge, his base of popular support would melt away.

To revive the earlier public enthusiasm, the President set out early in September on a speaking tour of the Middle and Far West. At Columbus, Ohio, the center of a region with many German-American families, he replied to the charge that Germany had been dealt with too harshly. The Versailles treaty, he said:

> . . . seeks to punish one of the greatest wrongs ever done in history, the wrong which Germany sought to do to the world and to civilization; and there ought to be no weak purpose with regard to the application of the punishment. She attempted an intolerable thing, and she must be made to pay for the attempt. The terms of the treaty are severe, but they are not unjust. I can testify that the men associated with me at the peace conference in Paris had it in their hearts to do justice and not wrong. But they knew, perhaps,

with a more vivid sense of what had happened than we could possibly know on this side of the water, the many solemn covenants which Germany had disregarded, the long preparation she had made to overwhelm her neighbors, and the utter disregard which she had shown for human rights, for the rights of women, of children, of those who were help-less. They had seen their lands devastated by an enemy that devoted himself not only to the effort at victory, but to the effort at terror—seeking to terrify the people whom he fought. And I wish to testify that they exercised restraint in the terms of this treaty. They did not wish to overwhelm any great nation. They acknowledged that Germany was a great nation, and they had no purpose of overwhelming the German people, but they did think that it ought to be burned into the consciousness of men forever that no people ought to permit its government to do what the German Government did.

In the last analysis, my fellow countrymen, as we in America would be the first to claim, a people are responsible for the acts of their government. If their government purposes things that are wrong, they ought to take measures to see to it that that purpose is not executed. Germany was self-governed; her rulers had not concealed the purposes that they had in mind, but they had deceived their people as to the character of the methods they were going to use, and I believe from what I can learn that there is an awakened consciousness in Germany itself of the deep iniquity of the thing that was attempted. . . . Throughout this treaty every term that was applied to Germany was meant, not to hu-miliate Germany, but to rectify the wrong that she had done.

In using this line of argument, Wilson departed some-what from his earlier position that the German government had not been representative of the German people. Perhaps he had to do so in order to defend the proposition that the treaty was harsh and yet not unjust.

There had been much criticism of the reparations clauses. At Paris Wilson had reluctantly agreed that Germany should, insofar as possible, pay all the costs of the war. He had also agreed that these costs should be interpreted to include bonuses and pensions to veterans. Since pensions could run on for years

and mount up to hundreds of billions of dollars, Germany was
to be saddled for all the foreseeable future with a debt larger
than she could ever pay. If the Allies chose to do so, they could
compel the Germans to hand over whatever they earned and
thus keep Germany forever a pauper. The young English econo-
mist John Maynard Keynes had resigned his post as adviser
to the British peace conference delegation and written an eloquent book, *The Economic Consequences of the Peace*, de-
nouncing the reparations clauses as likely to perpetuate economic instability and bring on new international friction. But
Wilson defended even these clauses. In his speech at Columbus, he said:

> Look even into the severe terms of reparation—for
> there was no indemnity. No indemnity of any sort was
> claimed, merely reparation, merely paying for the destruc-
> tion done, merely making good the losses so far as such
> losses could be made good which she had unjustly inflicted,
> not upon the governments, but upon the people whose rights
> she had trodden upon with absolute absence of everything
> that even resembled pity. There was no indemnity in this
> treaty, but there is reparation, and even in the terms of rep-
> aration a method is devised by which the reparation shall
> be adjusted to Germany's ability to pay it.
>
> I am astonished at some of the statements I hear
> made about this treaty. The truth is that they are made by
> persons who have not read the treaty or who, if they have
> read it, have not comprehended its meaning. There is a
> method of adjustment in that treaty by which the repara-
> tion shall not be pressed beyond the point which Germany
> can pay, but which will be pressed to the utmost point that
> Germany can pay—which is just, which is righteous. It
> would have been intolerable if there had been anything else.

During most of his tour, Wilson concentrated on the
Covenant, stressing the benefits it would bring. At Indianapolis, he declared:

> . . . the heart of the League of Nations covenant does not
> lie in any of the portions which have been discussed in pub-
> lic debate. The great bulk of the provisions of that covenant

contain these engagements and promises on the part of the states which undertake to become members of it: That in no circumstances will they go to war without first having done one or other of two things, without first either having submitted the question to arbitration, in which case they agree to abide by the results, or having submitted the question to discussion by the council of the League of Nations, in which case they will allow six months for the discussion and engage not to go to war until three months after the council has announced its opinion upon the subject under dispute. The heart of the covenant of the League is that the nations solemnly covenant not to go to war for nine months after a controversy becomes acute.

If there had been nine days of discussion, Germany would not have gone to war. If there had been nine days upon which to bring to bear the opinion of the world, the judgment of mankind, upon the purposes of those Governments, they never would have dared to execute those purposes. So that what it is important for us to remember is that when we sent those boys in khaki across the sea we promised them, we promised the world, that we would not conclude this conflict with a mere treaty of peace. We entered into solemn engagements with all the nations with whom we associated ourselves that we would bring about such a kind of settlement and such a concert of the purpose of nations that wars like this could not occur again. If this war has to be fought over again, then all our high ideals and purposes have been disappointed. . . .

Although up to that time Wilson had refrained from committing himself against specific reservations, he now did so. He used qualifying phrases. Nevertheless, he said, in effect, that he would fight any reservation touching the substance of Article 10:

Now, just a word about Article X. . . . The treaty was intended to destroy one system and substitute another. That other system was based upon the principle that no strong power need respect the territorial integrity or the political independence of any weak power. I need not confine the phraseology to that. It was based upon the principle that no power is obliged to respect the territorial integrity or the political independence of any other power if it has the force necessary to disregard it. So that Article X cuts at the very heart, and is the only instrument that will cut to the very heart, of the old system. Remember that if this covenant is adopted by the number of nations which it probably will be adopted by, it means that every nation except Germany and Turkey, . . . agree that they will respect and preserve against external aggression the territorial integrity and existing political independence of the other nations of the world. You would think from some of the discussions that the emphasis is on the word "preserve."

We are partners with the rest of the world in respecting the territorial integrity and political independence of others. They are all under solemn bonds themselves to respect and to preserve those things, and if they do not preserve them, if they do not respect them or preserve them, what happens? The council of the League then advises the several members of the League what it is necessary to do. I can testify from having sat at the board where the instrument was drawn that advice means advice. I supposed it did before I returned home, but I found some gentlemen doubted it. Advice means advice, and the advice can not be given without the concurrent vote of the representatives of the United States. "Ah," but somebody says, "suppose we are a party to the quarrel!" I can not suppose that, because I know that the United States is not going to disregard the territorial integrity or the political independence of any other nation, but for the sake of the argument suppose that we are a party. Very well then, the scrap is ours anyway. For what these gentlemen are afraid of is that we are going to get into trouble. If we are a party, we are in trouble already, and if we are not a party, we can control the advice of the council by our vote. To my mind, that is a little like an open and shut game! I am not afraid of advice which we give ourselves; and yet that is the whole of the bugaboo which these gentlemen have been parading before you.

The solemn thing about Article X is the first sentence, not the second sentence. The first sentence says that we will respect and preserve against external aggression the territorial integrity and existing political independence of other nations; and let me stop a moment on the words "external aggression." Why were they put in? Because every

man who sat at that board held that the right of revolution
was sacred and must not be interfered with. Any kind of a
row can happen inside and it is nobody's right to interfere.
The only thing that there is any right to object to or interfere with is external aggression, by some outside power un-
dertaking to take a piece of territory or to interfere with the
internal political arrangements of the country which is suffering from the aggression; because territorial integrity does
not mean that you can not invade another country; it means
that you can not invade it and stay there. I have not impaired the territorial integrity of your backyard if I walk
into it, but I very much impair it if I insist upon staying
there and will not get out, and the impairment of integrity
contemplated in this article is the kind of impairment as the
seizure of territory, as an attempt at annexation, as an attempt at continuing domination either of the territory
itself or of the methods of government inside that territory.

When you read Article X . . . you will see that it
is nothing but the inevitable, logical center of the whole
system of the covenant of the League of Nations, and I
stand for it absolutely. If it should ever in any important
respect be impaired, I would feel like asking the Secretary
of War to get the boys who went across the water to fight
together on some field where I could go and see them, and
I would stand up before them and say, "Boys, I told you before you went across the seas that this was a war against
wars, and I did my best to fulfill the promise, but I am
obliged to come to you in mortification and shame and say
I have not been able to fulfill the promise. You are be-
trayed. You fought for something that you did not get."
And the glory of the armies and the navies of the United
States is gone like a dream in the night, and there ensues
upon it, in the suitable darkness of the night, the night-
mare of dread which lay upon the nations before this war
came; and there will come sometime, in the vengeful Providence of God, another struggle in which, not a few hundred
thousand fine men from America will have to die, but as
many millions as are necessary to accomplish the final freedom of the peoples of the world.

Moving on westward from St. Louis, Wilson began to
shake off all restraint. In free-swinging style, he attacked first

one proposed reservation and then another. At Omaha he told his audience that he would "talk about these interesting things that we hear about that are called reservations." Defining a reservation as "an assent with a big but," he took up in order those that had most often been the subjects of newspaper speculation.

One of the changes Wilson had introduced in Paris gave a member of the League the right to withdraw after two years notice, provided it had fulfilled all obligations under the Covenant. Rumor had it that Lodge's Committee would recommend that the United States reserve the right to be the sole judge of whether or not it had met its obligations. Wilson commented of Senators who would support this reservation:

. . . They want to sit close to the door with their hands on the knob, and they want to say, "We are in this thing but we are in it with infinite timidity; we are in it only because you overpersuaded us and wanted to see us come in, and we are going to try this thing every now and then and see if it is locked, and just as soon as we see anything we don't like, we are going to scuttle." Now, what is the trouble? What are they afraid of? I want you to put this to every man you know who makes this objection, what is he afraid of? Is he afraid that when the United States withdraws it will not have fulfilled its international obligations? Is he willing to bring that indictment against this beloved country? My fellow citizens, we never did fail to fulfill an international obligation and, God guiding and helping us, we never will. I for one am not going to admit in any connection the slightest doubt that, if we ever choose to withdraw, we will then have fulfilled our obligations. If I make reservations, as they are called, about this, what do I do? This covenant does not set up any tribunal to judge whether we have fulfilled our obligations at that time or not. There is only one thing to restrain us, and that is the opinion of mankind. Are these gentlemen such poor patriots that they are afraid that the United States will cut a poor figure in the opinion of mankind? And do they think that they can bring this great people to withdraw from that League if at that time their withdrawal would be condemned by the opinion of mankind? We have always been at pains to earn the respect of mankind, and we shall always be at pains to retain it. I for one am too proud as an American to say that any doubt will ever hang around our right to withdraw upon the condition of the fulfillment of our international obligations.

Another of the amendments Wilson had secured in Paris had been the insertion in the Covenant of a new Article 21, which stated:

> Nothing in this Covenant shall be deemed to affect the validity of international engagements, such as treaties of arbitration or regional understandings like the Monroe Doctrine, for securing the maintenance of peace.

Some Senators wanted a reservation saying that the Monroe Doctrine was not a "regional understanding" and that the United States would not tolerate League interference in the Western Hemisphere. Wilson observed:

> They do not like the way in which the Monroe Doctrine is mentioned. Well, I would not stop on a question of style. The Monroe Doctrine is adopted. It is swallowed, hook, line, and sinker, and, being carefully digested into the central organism of the whole instrument, I do not care what language they use about it. The language is entirely satisfactory so far as I understand the English language. That puzzles me, my fellow citizens. The English language seems to have got some new meaning since I studied it that bothers these gentlemen. I do not know what dictionaries they resort to. I do not know what manuals of conscience they can possibly resort to. The Monroe Doctrine is expressly authenticated in this document, for the first time in history, by all the great nations of the world, and it was put there at our request.

In addition, Wilson remarked, some Senators wanted "a reservation enumerating certain questions as domestic questions which everybody on both sides of the water admits are domestic questions." He said vexedly:

> That seems to me, to say the least, to be a work of supererogation. It does not seem to me necessary to specify

what everybody admits, but they are so careful—I believe the word used to be "meticulous"—that they want to put in what is clearly implied in the whole instrument. . . . The conference at Paris will still be sitting when the Senate of the United States has acted upon this treaty. Perhaps I ought not to say that so confidently. No man, even in the secrets of Providence, can tell how long it will take the United States Senate to do anything, but I imagine that in the normal course of human fatigue the Senate will have acted upon this treaty before the conference in Paris gets through with the Austrian treaty and the Bulgarian treaty and the Turkish treaty. They will still be there on the job. Now—every lawyer will follow me in this—if you take a contract and change the words, even though you do not change the sense, you have to get the other parties to accept those words. Is not that true? Therefore every reservation will have to be taken back to all the signatories of this treaty, and I want you to notice that that includes Germany. We will have to ask Germany's consent to read this treaty the way we understand it. I want to tell you that we did not ask Germany's consent with regard to the meaning of any one of those terms while we were in Paris. We told her what they meant and said, "Sign here." Are there any patriotic Americans who desire the method changed? Do they want me to ask the . . . [Germans] if I may read the treaty the way it means but in words which the United States Senate thinks it ought to have been written in? You see, reservations come down to this, that they want to change the language of the treaty without changing its meaning and involve all the embarrassments. Because, let me say, there are indications—I am judging not from official dispatches but from the newspapers—that people are not in as good a humor over in Paris now as they were when I was there, and it is going to be more difficult to get agreement from now on than it was then. After dealing with some of those gentlemen I found that they were as ingenious as any American in attaching unexpected meanings to plain words, and, having gone through the mill on the existing language, I do not want to go through it again on changed language. . . .

Summing up, Wilson came out flatly against any reservations at all. He declared:

. . . we can not rewrite this treaty. We must take it or leave it, and gentlemen, after all the rest of the world has signed it, will find it very difficult to make any other kind of treaty. As I took the liberty of saying the other night, it is a case of "put up or shut up." The world can not breathe in the atmosphere of negations. The world can not deal with nations who say, "We won't play!" The world can not have anything to do with an arrangement in which every nation says, "We will take care of ourselves." Is it possible, my fellow citizens—is it possible, for the sinister thing has been suggested to me—that there is a group of individuals in this country who have conceived it as desirable that the United States should exercise its power alone, should arm for the purpose, should be ready for the enterprise, and should dominate the world by arms? There are indications that there are groups of citizens in this country who do not find that an unpalatable program. Are we going to substitute for Pan Germanism a sinister Pan Americanism? The thing is inconceivable. It is hideous. No man dare propose that in plain words to any American audience anywhere. The heart of this people is pure. The heart of this people is true. This great people loves liberty. It loves justice. It would rather have liberty and justice than wealth and power. It is the great idealistic force of history, and the idealism of America is what has made conquest of the spirits of men.

Going on through the northern plains, over the mountains to the state of Washington, down the Pacific coast, and back through the Southwest, Wilson hammered at the same points. In addition to scheduled speeches, he made innumerable pauses at whistle stops, preaching his message to whatever number would gather.

For Wilson himself, the trip was an ordeal. Though only sixty-one, he was frail in health. His doctors had insisted for years that he work no more than a few hours a day and take plenty of rest and exercise. In Washington he had generally followed this regimen. In Paris, however, he had not been able to do so. There he had worked day and night for weeks on end. A succession of colds and other complaints had resulted. He had never quite recovered from these, and now, once again, he was driving his physique as hard as it could be driven.

He began to suffer from headaches and sleeplessness. The White House doctor accompanying him urged that he give up the remainder of the tour. Wilson refused. By the time he reached Pueblo, Colorado, he was at the end of his resources. Nevertheless, before the audience that jammed the Opera House, he made one of the most eloquent speeches of the whole trip. He went over all that he had said earlier. About the Shantung question, he spoke bluntly:

> You have heard a great deal—something that was true and a great deal that was false—about that provision of the treaty which hands over to Japan the rights which Germany enjoyed in the Province of Shantung in China. In the first place, Germany did not enjoy any rights there that other nations had not already claimed. For my part, my judgment, my moral judgment, is against the whole set of concessions. They were all of them unjust to China, they ought never to have been exacted, they were all exacted by duress from a great body of thoughtful and ancient and helpless people. There never was any right in any of them. Thank God, America never asked for any, never dreamed of asking for any. But when Germany got this concession in 1898, the Government of the United States made no protest whatever. That was not because the Government of the United States was not in the hands of high-minded and conscientious men. It was. William McKinley was President and John Hay was Secretary of State—as safe hands to leave the honor of the United States in as any that you can cite. They made no protest because the state of international law at that time was that it was none of their business unless they could show that the interests of the United States were affected. . . I want you distinctly to understand that there is no thought of criticism in my mind. I am expounding to you a state of international law. Now, read Articles X and XI [of the Covenant]. You will see that international law is revolutionized by putting morals into it. Article X says that no member of the League, and that includes all these nations that have demanded these things unjustly of China, shall impair the territorial integrity or the political independence of any other member of the League. China is going to be a member of the League. Article XI says that any member of the League can call attention to anything

that is likely to disturb the peace of the world or the good understanding between nations, and China is for the first time in the history of mankind afforded a standing before the jury of the world. I, for my part, have a profound sympathy for China, and I am proud to have taken part in an arrangement which promises the protection of the world to the rights of China. The whole atmosphere of the world is changed by a thing like that, my fellow citizens. The whole international practice of the world is revolutionized.

From this, Wilson went on to speak more generally of Article 10, of the vision that he had carried with him to Paris, and of what he thought the treaty and the Covenant would accomplish:

. . . Article X strikes at the taproot of war. Article X is a statement that the very things that have always been sought in imperialistic wars are henceforth forgone by every ambitious nation in the world. I would have felt very lonely, my fellow countrymen, and I would have felt very much disturbed if, sitting at the peace table in Paris, I had supposed that I was expounding my own ideas. Whether you believe it or not, I know the relative size of my own ideas; I know how they stand related in bulk and proportion to the moral judgments of my fellow countrymen, and I proposed nothing whatever at the peace table at Paris that I had not sufficiently certain knowledge embodied the moral judgment of the citizens of the United States. I had gone over there with, so to say, explicit instructions. Don't you remember we laid down fourteen points which should contain the principles of the settlement? They were not my points. In every one of them I was conscientiously trying to read the thought of the people of the United States, and after I uttered those points I had every assurance given me that could be given me that they did speak the moral judgment of the United States and not my single judgment. Then when it came to that critical period just a little less than a year ago, when it was evident that the war was coming to its critical end, all the nations engaged in the war accepted those fourteen principles explicitly as the basis of the armistice and the basis of the peace. In those circumstances I crossed the ocean under bond to my own people and to the other governments with which I was dealing. The whole specification of the method of settlement was written down and accepted beforehand, and we were architects building on those specifications. . . .

Movingly, Wilson appealed for understanding of what the treaty meant to him:

Again and again, my fellow citizens, mothers who lost their sons in France have come to me and, taking my hand, have shed tears upon it not only, but they have added, "God bless you, Mr. President!" Why, my fellow citizens, should they pray God to bless me? I advised the Congress of the United States to create the situation that led to the death of their sons. I ordered their sons overseas. I consented to their sons being put in the most difficult parts of the battle line, where death was certain, as in the impenetrable difficulties of the forest of Argonne. Why should they weep upon my hand and call down the blessings of God upon me? Because they believe that their boys died for something that vastly transcends any of the immediate and palpable objects of the war. They believe, and they rightly believe, that their sons saved the liberty of the world. They believe that wrapped up with the liberty of the world is the continuous protection of that liberty by the concerted powers of all civilized people. They believe that this sacrifice was made in order that other sons should not be called upon for a similar gift—the gift of life, the gift of all that died. . . .

You will say, "Is the League an absolute guaranty against war?" No; I do not know any absolute guaranty against the errors of human judgment or the violence of human passion, but . . . I ask you this: If it is not an absolute insurance against war, do you want no insurance at all? Do you want nothing? Do you want not only no probability that war will not recur, but the probability that it will recur? The arrangements of justice do not stand of themselves, my fellow citizens. The arrangements of this treaty are just, but they need the support of the combined power of the great nations of the world. And they will have that support. Now that the mists of this great question have cleared away, I believe that men will see the truth, eye to eye and face to face. There is one thing that the

American people always rise to and extend their hand to, and that is the truth of justice and of liberty and of peace. We have accepted that truth and we are going to be led by it, and it is going to lead us, and through us the world, out into pastures of quietness and peace such as the world never dreamed of before.

After this supreme effort of oratory, Wilson could go on no longer. He returned to his train that night in a state of virtual collapse. His doctor now told him that he must cancel his remaining engagements. This time he did not refuse. The presidential train sped back to Washington. But even in the White House Wilson could not relax or sleep. His spent body did not have the resources for recovery, and, one night not long after his return, Mrs. Wilson found him prostrate on the floor. A stroke had paralyzed one whole side and reduced him to helpless invalidism.

After a few days he regained the ability to concentrate for a minute or two at a time. Soon he could be propped in a sitting position and with help could sign letters and state documents. But his family, his doctors, and the White House staff put a barrier between him and the world. He saw no one else, and his guardians, trying to keep him tranquil, would not let him receive up-to-the-minute news of how matters were progressing in the Senate.

There the Versailles treaty was at last on the floor. The Foreign Relations Committee had recommended a number of amendments and reservations. Each was the subject of exhaustive debate. One after another was discarded or modified until at last, by mid-November, the Republican mild reservationists and strong reservationists had agreed on fourteen reservations. One withheld assent to the Shantung arrangement. One stated that the United States, in the event of withdrawal from the League, should be the sole judge of whether or not it had fulfilled its obligations. One specified what domestic questions were to lie outside the competence of the League. One declared that the United States would "not submit to arbitra-

tion or to inquiry by the assembly or by the council of the
League of Nations . . . any questions which . . . depend upon
or relate to its long-established policy, commonly known as the
Monroe doctrine. . . ." Although most of the remainder were
relatively inconsequential, one struck directly at Article 10:

> The United States assumes no obligation to preserve the
> territorial integrity or political independence of any other
> country by the employment of its military or naval forces,
> its resources, or any form of economic discrimination, or
> to interfere in any way in controversies among nations,
> including all controversies relating to territorial integrity or
> political independence, whether members of the league or
> not, under the provisions of Article 10, or to employ the
> military or naval forces of the United States, under any
> article of the treaty for any purpose, unless in any particular
> case the Congress . . . shall, in the exercise of full liberty
> of action, by act or joint resolution so provide.

Had Wilson been in full possession of his faculties and
been exercising day-to-day leadership of the Senate Democrats,
he would have had to fight against this reservation or at least
fight for modification of it, for it undercut his whole concept
of collective security. Some of the other reservations, however,
he might have accepted, taking the ground that they were
unnecessary but meaningless. By doing so, he might have split
the Republicans, winning over the mild reservationists to a
coalition with the Democrats. But, isolated in his sickroom,
he had no judgment of the situation. When the day for a vote
came, he sent word to Democratic leaders on Capitol Hill that
they should stand fast against any and all reservations.

The Democrats obeyed his orders. When the Republicans moved for ratification with reservations, all but four
voted nay. The irreconcilables joined them, and the treaty in
that form went down to defeat 55 to 39. The Democratic
leadership then moved for ratification with no reservations at
all. The irreconcilables, of course, opposed this motion too.
So did all but one of the Republican reservationists. The vote

now was 53 against to 38 for. The Senate had refused its consent to the treaty of Versailles.

Another attempt was made in February, 1920. Wilson, though gradually regaining his strength, stuck to the position he had taken at the time of the first vote. (The fact that he was seriously thinking of running for a third term, calling for a national referendum on the League issue, suggests that his illness may have affected his mind.) Although a number of Democrats and moderate Republicans worked for a compromise, the necessary two thirds was still not forthcoming. Forty-nine voted for ratification with reservations; thirty-five (fourteen irreconcilables and twenty-one party-line Democrats) voted against. Thus vanished the last chance for the League that Wilson had envisioned.

The decision of the Senate has been the subject of many post-mortems by historians. When the postwar period proved to be nothing more than a long armistice, almost everyone looked back at 1919 with regret, feeling that if the United States had been in the League, World War II might not have come. Much recrimination was spilled on LaFollette and the other irreconcilables and especially on Lodge. In *Woodrow Wilson and the Great Betrayal*, Professor Thomas A. Bailey of Stanford righted the balance by pointing out that Wilson's stubbornness had had something to do with the outcome. He writes:

> In the final analysis the treaty was slain in the house of its friends rather than in the house of its enemies. In the final analysis it was not the two-thirds rule, or the "irreconcilables," or Lodge, or the "strong" and "mild reservationists," but Wilson and his docile following who delivered the fatal stab. . . .
>
> Wilson had said that the reservation to Article X was a knife thrust at the heart of the Covenant. Ironically, he parried this knife thrust, and stuck his own dagger, not into the heart of the Covenant, but into the entire treaty.

This was the supreme act of infanticide. With his own sickly hands Wilson slew his own brain child—or the one to which he had contributed so much. . . .

The preceding dogmatic observations are of course qualified by the phrase, "in the last analysis". . . .

Many elements entered into the legislative log jam. . . . Among them were isolationism, partisanship, senatorial prerogative, confusion, apathy, personal pride, and private feuds. No one of them was solely responsible for the pile-up. *But as the pile-up finally developed, there was only one lumberjack who could break it, and that was Woodrow Wilson.* If at any time before the final vote he had told the Senate Democrats to support the treaty with the Lodge reservations, or even if he had merely told them that they were on their own, the pact would almost certainly have been approved. So "in the last analysis" the primary responsibility for the failure in March rested with Wilson.

What about Lodge? If the treaty would have passed by Wilson's surrendering, is it not equally true that it would have passed by Lodge's surrendering?

The answer is probably "Yes," but the important point is that Lodge had far less responsibility for getting the treaty through than Wilson. If Lodge had yielded, he probably would have created a schism within his ranks. His ultimate responsibility was to keep the party from breaking to pieces, and in this he succeeded. Wilson's ultimate responsibility was to get the treaty ratified, and in this he failed. With Lodge, as with any truly partisan leader, the party comes before country; with the President the country should come before party, though unhappily it often does not. . . .

In March, as in November, all Wilson had to do was to send over Postmaster General Burleson to the Senate a few minutes before the final vote with the quiet word that the Democrats were to vote "Yea." The treaty would then have passed with the Lodge reservations, and Lodge could hardly have dared incur for himself or his party the odium of moving to reconsider for the purpose of screwing on more reservations. Had he tried to do so, the "mild reservationists" almost certainly would have blocked him. . . . Wilson gave orders that the treaty was to be killed in the Senate chamber. And there it died.

What happened in the election of 1920 and afterward is described by Professor Selig Adler in *The Isolationist Impulse:*

> It is tempting to speculate what might have happened had a presidential election not been just around the corner. . . . Wilson took the fatal step of asking the impossible —namely, that the election be "a great and solemn referendum" on the League. It would be difficult to imagine a more egregious error. The Republicans, who formed the ordinary majority, would be sure to pick up the President's gauntlet.
>
> The merits of the League question aside, the Wilsonians would have had the odds heavily against them. Eight years of Democratic rule had built up the usual resentments against the party in power. To this must be added the jaded disillusionment against the war and its inconveniences which were bound to react against the "ins." . . . When the verdict was in, the Democrats had gone down to inglorious defeat. Thinking men knew that it was not a mandate to bury the League. In the excitement of the campaign, however, so much had been said against the Covenant that it would prove impossible for the League to live down the calumny. There was room for a superficial judgment that the Democrats had thrown the dice on the issue and had failed to make their point. In history often what people think happened is more important than what actually did happen. The isolationists could say that the question had been posed, voted upon, and downed. . . .
>
> Thus the election of 1920 is of prime importance in the history of isolationism—not because of the way the people voted, but because of the dangerously simple popular interpretation of the result. . . . Millions of Americans had been given a promissory note . . . that a vote for Harding was a vote for the League with reservations. Would the note be made good? The President-elect gave the answer two days after the polls closed. He said that the question of joining was "now deceased," and in practice he was to regard the League issue as "dead as slavery." Thus blatantly ignoring the fact that he had beclouded the issue, and that there were many other more important factors involved,

Harding chose to interpret his tremendous victory as a popular mandate against the League. As even his commonplace mind must have suspected, a new world association was out of the question. To abandon the League, then, meant a return to isolationism. The Irreconcilables had won once more by coincidental circumstances. . . .

Paradoxically enough, the war that was to save the world for democracy set in motion a nationalist reaction which was inimical to the concept of global collective security. By March 4, 1921, when the florid Harding rode up Pennsylvania Avenue with the peaked Wilson, the great isolationist front had been formed. The coalition contained many different types of active members. There were liberals who wanted no part of a League that had been fashioned by the turncoat Wilson. Communists gave active help to the isolationists because they regarded the League as a dangerous derelict lying in the path that led to the economic unity of mankind. Strangely enough, many immigrants were isolationists simply because of strong European attachments. Some of the victorious Republicans, especially those of the eastern seaboard, wanted an international organization, but opposed the League scheme in its existing form. Borah, Johnson, LaFollette and their cohorts held tightly to a nineteenth-century form of nationalism, a concept which left no room for effective world organization. And there were the zealots who condemned everything foreign and who thought of our oceans as the Chinese had once thought of their wall. Important as all other factors were in evoking this mood of detachment, the nationalist creed was paramount. For that was a doctrine that immigrants and nativists, progressives and reactionaries, insular politicians and career diplomats had in common. Thus isolationism formed a common and seemingly solid ground amidst the drift of the twenties.

✶ ✶ ✶

In the 1890's the United States emerged as one of the great powers, and before and after the Spanish war Americans debated what policies they should follow now that their country was an equal of Great Britain, Germany, and the rest. Such men as Beveridge argued that it should conduct itself as European states did, getting into the scramble for colonies and positions of strength and advantage. Schurz and others contended that it should keep on behaving as it had when it was a small, second-rate power, concentrating on its own internal development and setting an example for the rest of the world. At the time, though the Philippines were taken, the debate seemed to end in a draw. The United States went no farther along the road of imperialism, but neither did it retreat to continental isolation.

Then in 1917 it went into the European war, apparently committed now to playing a great role in world affairs, not, it is true, the role that Beveridge had envisioned, but still one quite different from that of the past. And the treaty which Wilson brought back from Paris appeared to confirm the commitment. But the decision proved not to be final. Indeed, the votes in the Senate, followed by the election of 1920, turned back the clock. After 1920 the world was confronted with the spectacle of a power, now the greatest of all, renouncing any intention of making its force felt in other parts of the globe. National prohibition, introduced at the same time, was subsequently spoken of as a "noble experiment." The retreat to isolation deserves the same ambiguous characterization. It was, if anything, a nobler experiment, but it, too, was destined to fail.

Bibliography

Excellent general accounts of American diplomacy 1898–1919 may be found in Thomas A. Bailey, A *Diplomatic History of the American People* (6th ed.; New York: Appleton-Century-Crofts, 1958); Samuel F. Bemis, A *Diplomatic History of the United States* (4th ed.; New York: Holt, 1955); Foster R. Dulles, *America's Rise to World Power, 1898–1954* (New York: Harper, 1958; Harper Torchbooks paperback); Richard W. Leopold, *The Growth of American Foreign Policy* (New York: Knopf, 1962); Julius W. Pratt, A *History of United States Foreign Policy* (New York: Prentice-Hall, 1955); and Alexander DeConde, A *History of American Foreign Policy* (New York: Scribner, 1963). Of these Leopold and Dulles are the most detailed, as they emphasize the years since 1898.

Two pamphlets of the American Historical Association Service Center for Teachers of History are also helpful for interpretation: Alexander DeConde, *New Interpretations in American Foreign Policy* (1957) and Ernest May, *American Intervention: 1917 and 1941* (1960).

On the Spanish-American War and the Philippine question, see Foster R. Dulles, *Imperial America* (New York: McGraw-Hill, 1956); Ernest R. May, *Imperial Democracy: The Emergence of America as a Great Power* (New York: Harcourt, 1961); Walter Millis, *The Martial Spirit* (Boston: Houghton Mifflin, 1931); Julius W. Pratt, *Expansionists of 1898* (Baltimore: Johns Hopkins University Press, 1936); and Julius W. Pratt, *America's Colonial Experiment* (New York: Prentice-Hall, 1950). Pratt revises the earlier economic interpretation of the causes of the war. Millis refuses to take the war seriously.

For humorous observations on the period of the war, see Louis Filler, ed., *The World of Mr. Dooley* (New York: Collier Books, 1962). There is a useful collection of sources in Ernest R. May, ed., "Overseas Expansion: The Coming of the War with Spain, 1895–1898," in Merrill D. Peterson and Leonard W. Levy, eds., *Major Crises in American History* (New York: Harcourt, 1962).

For diplomacy between the war with Spain and the First World War, see George E. Mowry, *The Era of Theodore Roosevelt* (New York: Harper, 1958; Harper Torchbooks paperback); Howard K. Beale, *Theodore Roosevelt and America's Rise to World Power* (Baltimore: John Hopkins University Press, 1956; Collier Books paperback); William H. Harbaugh, *Power and Responsibility* (New York: Farrar, Straus, 1961); and Henry F. Pringle, *Theodore Roosevelt: A Biography* (New York: Harcourt, 1931; Harvest Books paperback). Mowry is fairer in his treatment of Roosevelt than is Pringle. Harbaugh's is the most recent one-volume biography of Roosevelt.

On intervention in World War I, see Edward H. Buehrig, *Woodrow Wilson and the Balance of Power* (Bloomington: University of Indiana Press, 1955); John M. Blum, *Woodrow Wilson and the Politics of Morality* (Boston: Little, Brown, 1956; Little, Brown paperback); Arthur S. Link, *Woodrow Wilson* (3 vols. to date, Princeton, N.J.: Princeton University Press, 1947—); Arthur S. Link, *Woodrow Wilson and the Progressive Era, 1910–1917* (New York: Harper, 1954; Harper Torchbooks paperback); Arthur S. Link, *Wilson the Diplomatist* (Baltimore: Johns Hopkins University Press, 1957); Ernest R. May, *The World War and American Isolation, 1914–1917* (Cambridge, Mass.: Harvard University Press, 1959); Walter Millis, *The Road to War, 1914–1917* (Boston: Houghton Mifflin, 1935); and Charles Seymour, *The World War and American Neutrality* (Baltimore: Johns Hopkins University Press, 1934). For source material see Ernest R. May, ed., *The Coming of War, 1917* (Berkeley Readings in American History; Chicago: Rand McNally, 1963).

On the defeat of the Treaty of Versailles and the retreat to isolationism, see Selig Adler, *The Isolationist Impulse: Its Twentieth Century Reaction* (New York: Abelard-Schuman, 1957; Collier Books paperback, 1961); Thomas A. Bailey, *Woodrow Wilson and the Lost Peace* (New York: Macmillan, 1944); Thomas A. Bailey, *Woodrow Wilson and the Great Betrayal* (New York: Macmillan, 1945); and Henry Cabot Lodge, *The Senate and the League of Nations* (New York: Scribner, 1925). For sources, see Ernest R. May, ed., "World War I: Wilson and the Peace of Versailles, 1919," in Peterson and Levy, eds., *Major Crises in American History* (New York: Harcourt, 1962).

Index